CONSTITUTIONAL LAW: THE RELIGION CLAUSES

Second Edition

by

DANIEL O. CONKLE
Robert H. McKinney Professor of Law
Indiana University Bloomington

TURNING POINT SERIES®

FOUNDATION PRESS
2009

THOMSON

WEST

Turning Point Series is a registered trademark used herein under license.

© 2003 FOUNDATION PRESS
© 2009 By THOMSON REUTERS/FOUNDATION PRESS

195 Broadway, 9th Floor
New York, NY 10007
Phone Toll Free 1–877–888–1330
Fax (212) 367–6799
foundation-press.com

Printed in the United States of America

ISBN 978–1–59941–341–9

TEXT IS PRINTED ON 10% POST
CONSUMER RECYCLED PAPER

TURNING POINT SERIES

CIVIL PROCEDURE
- *Civil Procedure: Class Actions* by Linda S. Mullenix, University of Texas (Available 2010)
- *Civil Procedure: Economics of Civil Procedure* by Robert G. Bone, Boston University (2003)
- *Civil Procedure: Preclusion in Civil Actions* by David L. Shapiro, Harvard University (2001)
- *Civil Procedure: Territorial Jurisdiction and Venue* by Kevin M. Clermont, Cornell (1999)

CONSTITUTIONAL LAW
- *Constitutional Law: The Commerce Clause* by Dan T. Coenen, University of Georgia (2004)
- *Constitutional Law: Equal Protection* by Louis M. Seidman, Georgetown University (2003)
- *Constitutional Law: The Religion Clauses, Second Edition* by Daniel O. Conkle, Indiana University, Bloomington (2009)

CRIMINAL LAW
- *Criminal Law: Model Penal Code* by Markus D. Dubber, State University of New York, Buffalo (2002)

ENVIRONMENTAL LAW

- *Environmental Law: RCRA, CERCLA, and the Management of Hazardous Waste* by John S. Applegate, Indiana University, Bloomington and Jan G. Laitos, University of Denver Sturm College of Law (2006)

FEDERAL COURTS

- *Federal Courts: Habeas Corpus* by Larry W. Yackle, Boston University (2003)

INTERNATIONAL LAW

- *International Law: United States Foreign Relations Law* by Phillip R. Trimble, UCLA (2002)

JURY AND TRIAL PRACTICE

- *The Jury Process* by Nancy S. Marder, Chicago–Kent College of Law (2005)

LEGISLATION

- *Legislation: Statutory Interpretation:* Twenty Questions by Kent R. Greenawalt, Columbia University (1999)

PROPERTY

- *Property: Takings* by David Dana, Northwestern University and Thomas Merrill, Northwestern University (2002)

CORPORATE/SECURITIES

- *Securities Law: Insider Trading, Second Edition* by Stephen Bainbridge, UCLA (2007)

TORTS

- *Torts: Proximate Cause* by Joseph A. Page, Georgetown University (2003)

*For my parents, Louis and Berniece Conkle, who
introduced me to the law and
to religion.*

*

PREFACE TO THE SECOND EDITION

This book provides a theoretical framework for understanding and evaluating the Supreme Court's constitutional decisionmaking under the Religion Clauses of the First Amendment. It is intended primarily for legal scholars, law students, and lawyers. At the same time, the book also may be useful to a broader audience, including students in other disciplines and citizens wishing to educate themselves on this important topic of contemporary concern.

The Supreme Court's decisionmaking under the Religion Clauses is highly controversial. It also is complicated and confusing. But as this book explains, the Court's decisionmaking can be seen to have a certain coherency, if only as the product of a complex weighing of various and sometimes conflicting constitutional values.

The book begins in Chapter 1 with an introductory discussion. Chapter 2 addresses the original understanding of the Religion Clauses (and of the Fourteenth Amendment, which has been used to extend the Religion Clauses to the states), only to conclude that the original understanding cannot explain the Supreme Court's decisions. Chapter 3 then offers a brief history of American religious liberty, from the founding to the present. It suggests that the Court's decisionmaking under the Religion

Clauses has been influenced by a variety of embedded and evolving constitutional values—values such as religious equality and voluntarism; the protection of religious identity; the protection of religion from governmental contamination and of government from improper religious involvement; and the preservation of traditional governmental practices. This discussion sets the stage for the remainder of the book, which continually returns to these values as it explains and evaluates all of the major facets of the Court's constitutional doctrine.

Turning to a direct discussion of that doctrine, Chapter 4 addresses fundamental issues common to both the Free Exercise and Establishment Clauses, including the definition of "religion" and the general principle of nondiscrimination, which plays a powerful role in the Supreme Court's decisionmaking. Chapter 5 examines the Court's Free Exercise jurisprudence, emphasizing the role of discrimination in this context and highlighting the Court's treatment of claims for religion-based exemptions from nondiscriminatory laws. Chapter 6, the most extensive chapter in the book, confronts the various and complex ingredients of the Court's Establishment Clause doctrine. Like the book overall, this chapter proceeds from the general to the specific. Thus, it initially addresses the general Establishment Clause standards of *Lemon v. Kurtzman*, the endorsement test, and the coercion test, as well as the basic doctrinal concepts of tradition and accommodation. It then examines more specific areas of concern, including religion and the public schools; religious symbolism in other contexts; and public aid to religious schools, organizations, and individuals. The final chapter, Chapter 7, offers some concluding observations, and it includes a brief look to the future.

This second edition incorporates and discusses important developments of the last five years, including the Supreme Court's controversial Free Exercise decision in *Locke v. Davey*, its decisions upholding and applying recent religious liberty statutes, and its divided rulings concerning public displays of the Ten Commandments. It also addresses the potential significance of the Court's recent membership changes, with Chief Justice Roberts replacing Chief Justice Rehnquist and Justice Alito replacing Justice O'Connor.

DANIEL O. CONKLE

Bloomington, Indiana
October 2008

*

ABOUT THE AUTHOR

Daniel O. Conkle is the Robert H. McKinney Professor of Law at Indiana University Bloomington, where he also serves as an Adjunct Professor of Religious Studies and as a Nelson Poynter Scholar at the Poynter Center for the Study of Ethics and American Institutions. A graduate of the Ohio State University College of Law, Professor Conkle clerked for Judge Edward Allen Tamm of the U.S. Court of Appeals for the D.C. Circuit and practiced with the Cincinnati law firm of Taft, Stettinius & Hollister before joining the Indiana University faculty in 1983. Professor Conkle has published extensively on constitutional law and theory, religious liberty, and the role of religion in American law, politics, and public life.

*

TABLE OF CONTENTS

XIII

Table of Contents

Constitutional Law: The Religion Clauses

*

CHAPTER 1

INTRODUCTION

The first words of the First Amendment refer not to speech, but to religion: "Congress shall make no law respecting an establishment of religion, or prohibiting the free exercise thereof...." Simple enough, or so the framers might have thought.

To be sure, the basic principle of religious liberty emerged in the founding period, and, in one form or another, it has prevailed ever since. The precise meaning of religious liberty, however, was contested even in the founding period, and the passage of time has only made the issues more difficult. The First Amendment's Religion Clauses include the Free Exercise Clause and the Establishment Clause. But what does it mean to protect the free exercise of religion? Are religious practices protected from general laws, or only from religious discrimination? What if the religious practices cause harm? Are all acts of religious conscience included? And what makes an act "religious" in the first place? What about the Establishment Clause? Disestablishment precludes the formal recognition of a government church, but what else? Does it bar the government from promoting particular religions, or even religion in general? Even through non-coercive, purely symbolic actions? Are public schools precluded not

1

only from leading students in prayer, but also from permitting students to conduct their own prayers at school functions or during after-school meetings? Can the government extend nondiscriminatory financial support to private religious schools and organizations? May it accommodate the free exercise of religion by exempting religious practices from general laws, or would that amount to a forbidden establishment?

More generally, by what criteria, and by what process of decisionmaking, should these sorts of questions be confronted and resolved? Viewed through the lens of the First Amendment, they are questions of constitutional law and, as a result, questions ultimately for the Supreme Court. On its face, however, the relevant constitutional text is impossibly vague and general. It requires interpretation. The Court might—and does—look behind the text to the original understanding of the Religion Clauses, but, as we will see in Chapter 2, the original understanding itself is indeterminate. It does not begin to resolve the issues of religious liberty that have engaged the modern Court.

Although the Supreme Court may be loath to admit it, the Religion Clauses in fact have required creative interpretation. This value-laden process of decisionmaking, however, has not been purely subjective. The Court's creative interpretation has been guided in part by the text and original understanding of the Religion Clauses, but in far greater part by the Court's more general identification and protection of constitutional values. Thus, in interpreting the Religion Clauses, the Court has protected a variety of constitutional values—values deeply embedded in our political and cultural history, if not in the original understanding as such, and values emerging and evolving over time. In the jargon of constitutional theory, the Court's interpretive methodology might fairly be described as "nonoriginalist"; that is, the Court has moved beyond the text and original understanding, interpreting the Religion Clauses in a manner that has reflected not only American history, but also contemporary societal conditions and values.

To critics, the Supreme Court has been all too "creative" in its interpretations, producing a body of constitutional doctrine that is widely regarded as confusing, if not chaotic. On close examination, however, the Court's doctrine can be seen to have a certain coherency, if only as the product of a complex evaluation of various and sometimes competing constitutional values. In Chapter 3, we will examine the primary constitutional values that are at work—values such as religious equality and voluntarism; the protection of religious identity; the protection of religion from governmental contamination and of government from improper religious involvement; and the preservation of traditional governmental practices. The book will return to these values time and again as it explains and evaluates the various components of the Court's doctrine.

Turning to a direct discussion of that doctrine, Chapter 4 will address fundamental issues common to both of the Religion Clauses, including the definition of "religion" and the general principle of nondiscrimination, which, as we will see, plays a powerful role in the Court's decisionmaking. Chapter 5 will examine the Court's Free Exercise jurisprudence, emphasizing the role of discrimination in this context and highlighting the Court's vacillation concerning claims for religion-based exemptions from nondiscriminatory laws. Chapter 6, by far the longest chapter in the book, will confront the various and complex ingredients of the Court's Establishment Clause doctrine. Like the book overall, this chapter will proceed from the general to the specific. Thus, it will initially address basic concepts and doctrinal tests that undergird the Court's Establishment Clause cases in general. It then will examine more specific areas of concern, including religion and the public schools; religious symbolism in other contexts; and public aid to religious schools, organizations, and individuals.

The final chapter, Chapter 7, will offer some concluding observations, and it will include a brief look toward the future. The Supreme Court's doctrine under the Religion Clauses has evolved over time, and there is no reason to doubt that this evolution will continue.

Chapter 2

The Original Understanding

In 1789, the First Congress convened in New York City. The Constitution had taken effect, but, in the course of ratification, some states and citizens had expressed reservations. Indeed, two states, Rhode Island and North Carolina, had declined to join the union. Those who objected feared that in the absence of a Bill of Rights, the new general government might overstep its authority, intruding on the rights of individuals and the powers of the states. In response to these concerns, James Madison, a prominent member of the House of Representatives, proposed a series of constitutional amendments, including the following provision on the subject of religion: "The civil rights of none shall be abridged on account of religious belief or worship, nor shall any national religion be established, nor shall the full and equal rights of conscience be in any manner, or on any pretext, infringed."[1]

Over the course of several months, Madison's proposals were considered and revised, first in the House and then in the Senate. The provision con-

1. 1 Annals of Cong. 434 (Joseph Gales ed., 1789). Madison also proposed a separate provision, directed to the states as opposed to the national government, that likewise would have protected "the equal rights of conscience." *Id.* at 435.

5

cerning religion underwent various changes in phrasing. At one point, for example, the provision was amended to state that "Congress shall make no laws touching religion, or infringing the rights of conscience."[2] At another, it was revised to read that "Congress shall make no law establishing articles of faith or a mode of worship, or prohibiting the free exercise of religion."[3] The substantive significance of these changes is not entirely clear. More generally, the congressional record is sparse. In the House, the recorded debate on the religion provision was brief and inconclusive, and the Senate debate was not reported at all. Ultimately, after a House–Senate conference, Congress agreed to the religion provision, now in the version that we know as the Religion Clauses: "Congress shall make no law respecting an establishment of religion, or prohibiting the free exercise thereof."

Congress having approved the Religion Clauses, and the Bill of Rights generally, the amendments were submitted to the states for their consideration. Under Article V of the Constitution, the congressional action was no more than a proposal. To be enacted, the amendments required ratification. Some two years later, in 1791, three fourths of the states had ratified. Article V was satisfied, and the Bill of Rights—including the Religion Clauses of the

2. *Id.* at 731.

3. 1 Documentary History of the First Federal Congress of the United States of America 166 (Linda Grant De Pauw ed., 1972) (Senate Journal).

First Amendment—became part of the Constitution.

The Supreme Court and the "Virginia Understanding"

Remarkably enough, the Supreme Court had no occasion to interpret the Religion Clauses for almost 90 years. Finally, in 1879, the Court decided *Reynolds v. United States*.[4] In *Reynolds*, the Court held that the Free Exercise Clause did not protect Mormons from a federal statute forbidding polygamy. More important for present purposes, the Court purported to describe and give effect to the original understanding of the Religion Clauses. In so doing, however, the Court invoked pre-constitutional history, including especially the experience in Virginia:

Before the adoption of the Constitution, attempts were made in some of the colonies and States to legislate not only in respect to the establishment of religion, but in respect to its doctrines and precepts as well. The people were taxed, against their will, for the support of religion, and sometimes for the support of particular sects to whose tenets they could not and did not subscribe. Punishments were prescribed for a failure to attend upon public worship, and sometimes for entertaining heretical opinions. The controversy upon this general subject was animated in

4. 98 U.S. 145 (1879).

many of the States, but seemed at last to culminate in Virginia.[5]

In Virginia, the Court noted, James Madison and Thomas Jefferson had led a fight for disestablishment and religious freedom, and they had prevailed. In his famous *Memorial and Remonstrance Against Religious Assessments*, Madison had argued forcefully that religion and its exercise are not within the cognizance of civil government.[6] The Virginia House of Delegates had agreed, not only rejecting a system of tax-supported religion, but going on to adopt a competing legislative proposal from Jefferson, his celebrated Virginia Act for Religious Freedom.[7] In *Reynolds*, the Court cited the Virginia Act's preamble for the proposition that religious freedom, properly understood, protects "the profession or propagation of [religious] principles," but not "overt acts against peace and good order."[8] The Court went on to note Madison's role in the First Congress, and, although Jefferson had no such involvement, the Court nonetheless quoted and relied upon a letter that Jefferson wrote some years later to the Danbury Baptist Association:

5. *Id.* at 162–63.

6. *See* James Madison, Memorial and Remonstrance Against Religious Assessments (June 20, 1785), *reprinted in* 5 The Founders' Constitution 82 (Philip B. Kurland & Ralph Lerner eds., 1987).

7. Virginia Act for Religious Freedom, Va. Code Ann. § 57–1 (2008) (enacted Jan. 16, 1786).

8. *Reynolds*, 98 U.S. at 163 (quoting preamble to Virginia Act for Religious Freedom).

Believing with you that religion is a matter which lies solely between man and his God; that he owes account to none other for his faith or his worship; that the legislative powers of the government reach actions only, and not opinions,—I contemplate with sovereign reverence that act of the whole American people which declared that their Legislature should "make no law respecting an establishment of religion or prohibiting the free exercise thereof," thus building a wall of separation between church and State. Adhering to this expression of the supreme will of the nation in behalf of the rights of conscience, I shall see with sincere satisfaction the progress of those sentiments which tend to restore man to all his natural rights, convinced he has no natural right in opposition to his social duties.[9]

Calling Jefferson "an acknowledged leader of the advocates of the measure," the Court concluded that the opinion he expressed in this letter "may be accepted almost as an authoritative declaration of the scope and effect of the amendment thus secured." In thereby equating Jefferson's understanding with the original understanding, the Court suggested that the Establishment Clause erected a "wall of separation" between church and state. As for the Free Exercise Clause, the Court read Jefferson, and therefore the original understanding, to mean that "Congress was deprived of all legislative

9. *Reynolds*, 98 U.S. at 164 (quoting Letter from Thomas Jefferson to Danbury Baptist Association (Jan. 1, 1802)). Jefferson's letter is reprinted in 5 The Founders' Constitution, *supra* note 6, at 96.

power over mere opinion, but was left free to reach actions which were in violation of social duties or subversive of good order."[10]

After its 1879 decision in *Reynolds*, the Supreme Court's encounters with the Religion Clauses were no more than sporadic for another 60 years, until 1940, when the Court decided *Cantwell v. Connecticut*.[11] *Cantwell* held that the Free Exercise Clause, applicable by its terms only to federal action, would be applied to the states as well, based on the Court's determination that the Fourteenth Amendment (which explicitly addresses the states) "incorporated" the provisions of the Free Exercise Clause. *Cantwell* suggested that the Establishment Clause was likewise incorporated, and the Court so ruled a few years later, in its 1947 decision in *Everson v. Board of Education*.[12] The first of many modern cases challenging financial aid programs, *Everson* announced a broad and general explanation of the Establishment Clause:

> The "establishment of religion" clause of the First Amendment means at least this: Neither a state nor the Federal Government can set up a church. Neither can pass laws which aid one religion, aid all religions, or prefer one religion over another. Neither can force nor influence a person to go to or to remain away from church against his will or force him to profess a belief or disbelief in any religion. No person can be pun-

10.   *Reynolds*, 98 U.S. at 164.

11.   310 U.S. 296 (1940).

12.   330 U.S. 1 (1947).

ished for entertaining or professing religious beliefs or disbeliefs, for church attendance or non-attendance. No tax in any amount, large or small, can be levied to support any religious activities or institutions, whatever they may be called, or whatever form they may adopt to teach or practice religion. Neither a state nor the Federal Government can, openly or secretly, participate in the affairs of any religious organizations or groups and vice versa. In the words of Jefferson, the clause against establishment of religion by law was intended to erect "a wall of separation between church and State."[13]

As it had done decades earlier in *Reynolds*, the Court in *Everson* claimed that its interpretation was grounded in the original understanding of the Religion Clauses, and it tied that original understanding to pre-constitutional history, to the Virginia experience, and to the views of James Madison and Thomas Jefferson. According to the Court, the people of Virginia had "reached the conviction that individual religious liberty could be achieved best under a government which was stripped of all power to tax, to support, or otherwise to assist any or all religions, or to interfere with the beliefs of any religious individual or group."[14] And "the provisions of the First Amendment, in the drafting and adoption of which Madison and Jefferson played such leading roles, had the same objective and were intended to provide the same protection against

13. *Id.* at 15–16.

14. *Id.* at 11.

governmental intrusion on religious liberty as the [Virginia Act for Religious Freedom]."[15]

As we will see in later chapters, the Supreme Court, in the years since *Everson*, has struggled mightily as it has formulated doctrinal tests, revised them, and applied them to specific issues. The Court often has been deeply divided, and its decisions have generated tremendous controversy and debate. Through it all, however, the Supreme Court has not departed from the central interpretive claims set forth in *Reynolds* and reaffirmed in *Everson*: that the Court's decisions are properly based on the original understanding of the Religion Clauses and that the original understanding itself is based on pre-constitutional history, especially in Virginia, with the views of Madison and Jefferson leading the way. Let us call this the "Virginia understanding" of the Religion Clauses.

Some modern justices have challenged the Court's position. Chief Justice Rehnquist, for example, forthrightly rejected the Virginia understanding. In his dissenting opinion in *Wallace v. Jaffree*,[16] Rehnquist noted that Jefferson was not even in the United States when the First Amendment was proposed and ratified and therefore hardly could have played a "leading role" in its adoption. Rehnquist

15. *Id.* at 13. Although the Court in *Everson* split 5–4 in resolving the particular case at hand, the dissenters' historical analysis was similar to the majority's, and they reached a similar general conclusion about the original understanding of the Religion Clauses.

16. 472 U.S. 38 (1985). Rehnquist was an Associate Justice, not the Chief Justice, at the time of this decision.

did not deny the influential role of Madison, but he argued that as a member of the First Congress, Madison was "speaking as an advocate of sensible legislative compromise, not as an advocate of incorporating the Virginia Statute of Religious Liberty into the United States Constitution."[17] Focusing especially on the Establishment Clause and referring to the "wall of separation" as a "misleading metaphor,"[18] Rehnquist argued that Madison and the First Congress did not mean to disturb the then-common belief that it was proper for the government to further and support religion. According to Rehnquist, Madison intended the Establishment Clause "to prohibit the establishment of a national religion, and perhaps to prevent discrimination among sects. He did not see it as requiring neutrality on the part of government between religion and irreligion."[19]

Justice Souter, by contrast, has defended the Court's reliance on the Virginia understanding. In his concurring opinion in *Lee v. Weisman*,[20] Souter rejected Rehnquist's historical arguments, and he reaffirmed, on historical grounds, the principle that "the Establishment Clause forbids not only state

17. *Id.* at 98 (Rehnquist, J., dissenting).

18. *Id.* at 92.

19. *Id.* at 98. Justices Scalia and Thomas have offered historical arguments concerning the Establishment Clause that are sympathetic to those of Chief Justice Rehnquist. *See, e.g.*, Lee v. Weisman, 505 U.S. 577, 632–36, 640–42 (1992) (Scalia, J., dissenting); Rosenberger v. Rector & Visitors of the Univ. of Va., 515 U.S. 819, 852–63 (1995) (Thomas, J., concurring).

20. 505 U.S. 577 (1992).

practices that 'aid one religion ... or prefer one religion over another,' but also those that 'aid all religions.' "[21] Focusing on the proceedings of the First Congress, Souter offered a detailed, step-by-step account of the various revisions in Madison's original proposal. Noting that the final language of the Establishment Clause was broader and more categorical than some of the earlier alternatives, Souter concluded that the sequence of congressional revisions, combined with the ultimate text, confirm that the First Congress intended to prohibit even nonpreferential aid to religion. He argued that the framers were aware of nonpreferential as well as preferential establishments, and that they had intended to condemn them both, just as Madison and Jefferson had done in Virginia.[22]

With respect to the Free Exercise Clause, the Supreme Court likewise has continued to invoke the original understanding, and it has traced that understanding to pre-constitutional history, to Virginia, and to James Madison and Thomas Jefferson. In the Court's initial encounter with the Free Exercise Clause, as noted earlier, it held in *Reynolds* that the Clause did not protect the Mormon practice of polygamy from the operation of a general federal prohibition. *Reynolds* relied on Thomas Jefferson

21. *Id.* at 609–10 (Souter, J., concurring) (quoting *Everson*).

22. *See id.* at 612–16. Justice Souter's analysis was derived in part from Douglas Laycock, *"Nonpreferential" Aid to Religion: A False Claim About Original Intent*, 27 Wm. & Mary L. Rev. 875 (1986). *See also Rosenberger*, 515 U.S. at 868–72 (Souter, J., dissenting) (reiterating that the Religion Clauses, including especially the Establishment Clause, reflect the views of Madison and Jefferson, as expressed in Virginia).

for the proposition that the Free Exercise Clause protects religious beliefs and opinions, but not religious conduct that violates general social duties. To read the Clause to exempt religious conduct from a general, nondiscriminatory law, the Court suggested, would improperly permit a religious believer "to become a law unto himself."[23] In more recent decades, as we will see in Chapter 5, the Court has wavered on the question of whether the Free Exercise Clause exempts religious conduct from general laws. In 1990, however, the Court declared in *Employment Division v. Smith*[24] that it was reverting largely to the position that it had first announced in *Reynolds*, namely, that the Clause does not require such exemptions.

The Court was deeply divided on the exemptions issue in *Smith*, and it remains divided on this question, but justices on both sides invoke the same central claims: that they wish to honor the original understanding of the Free Exercise Clause and that their own point of view concerning exemptions is supported not only by the constitutional text, but also by pre-constitutional history and by the Virginia experience. Writing for the majority in *Smith*, Justice Scalia relied on his interpretation of the Court's precedents, including *Reynolds*, but he also focused on the text of the First Amendment. In so doing, he conceded that the "exercise of religion" includes religious conduct, but he argued that general regulations of conduct are not laws "prohibiting the free exercise [of religion]" and therefore do not violate the Free Exercise Clause. In his concur-

23. Reynolds v. United States, 98 U.S. 145, 167 (1879).
24. 494 U.S. 872 (1990).

ring opinion in *City of Boerne v. Flores*,[25] Scalia supplemented his textual claim by arguing that *Smith*'s rejection of constitutionally required exemptions was consistent with pre-constitutional understandings in the various colonies and states, including Virginia, and that it honored the views of Madison and Jefferson alike. In her dissenting opinion in *Boerne*, by contrast, Justice O'Connor contended that *Smith*'s rejection of constitutionally required exemptions not only contradicted prior precedents, but also dishonored the text and original understanding of the Free Exercise Clause. And just what did she cite in support of her position?—pre-constitutional history, of course, including especially that of Virginia, and the views of Madison and Jefferson alike![26]

The Original Understanding and Federalism

In evaluating the justices' debates concerning the original understanding,[27] we need to begin

25. 521 U.S. 507, 537–44 (1997) (Scalia, J., concurring in part).

26. *See id.* at 548–65 (O'Connor, J., dissenting); *see also Smith*, 494 U.S. at 892–903 (O'Connor, J., concurring in the judgment). For further exploration of the original understanding of the Free Exercise Clause, especially as it relates to exemptions, compare Michael W. McConnell, *The Origins and Historical Understanding of Free Exercise of Religion*, 103 Harv. L. Rev. 1409 (1990), with Philip A. Hamburger, *A Constitutional Right of Religious Exemption: An Historical Perspective*, 60 Geo. Wash. L.Rev. 915 (1992).

27. Some of the analysis that follows is adapted from Daniel O. Conkle, *Toward a General Theory of the Establishment Clause*, 82 Nw. U. L. Rev. 1113, 1129–42 (1988).

with some general observations about the Supreme Court's enforcement of constitutional values, including "originalist" values. The Court's enforcement of constitutional values is controversial because it frustrates the ordinary process of (representative) majoritarian self-government; at bottom, it permits an unelected Supreme Court to override the policy judgments of elected officials. When justices rely on the original understanding of the Constitution, however, they are claiming an "originalist" justification for their decisionmaking. Thus, they contend, they are protecting originalist values—values that may conflict with contemporary majoritarian policies, but values that, at some point in the past, were themselves placed in the Constitution by a majoritarian process, the process of constitutional enactment. The majoritarian foundation of originalism means that appeals to the original understanding must be appeals to the *collective* intentions of the framers and ratifiers of the relevant constitutional provision.[28] Under this

28. Recent academic literature sometimes refers to a more general sense of "original public meaning." *See, e.g.,* Vasan Kesavan & Michael Stokes Paulsen, *The Interpretive Force of the Constitution's Secret Drafting History*, 91 Geo. L.J. 1113, 1127–48 (2003). But the "original understanding" of the framers and ratifiers—their collective understanding and intentions in adopting a constitutional provision—is the more appropriate focus because it more directly honors the majoritarian foundation of

analysis, the values originally embodied in the Religion Clauses are those that the framers and ratifiers collectively—and not merely Madison or any other individual—understood and intended the Clauses to embrace. Conversely, if the inclusion of any value would have caused the provision to fail in the First Congress or in the ratification process, that value cannot be said to be part of the original understanding.

It can be exceedingly difficult, if not impossible, to determine the original understanding of a provision in the Bill of Rights. The evidentiary materials are woefully incomplete, and it is difficult to determine the relevance and relative weight of the various types of evidence that do exist. The Religion Clauses fall prey to these evidentiary and analytical problems and, as a result, it is difficult to tell precisely what the framers and ratifiers had in mind. In this instance, however, the difficulty is compounded by a fundamental problem: focusing, as we must, on the collective intentions of the framers and ratifiers, the evidence suggests that the Religion Clauses simply were not designed to be used—as they are today—as a statement of general principles concerning religious liberty and the relationship between religion and government. Rather, they were designed to address these issues exclusively as to congressional action and, as such, they

originalism. In any event, there is no indication that the original public meaning is any different than the original understanding of the framers and ratifiers in the context at hand, so shifting the focus to original public meaning would not change any of the basic conclusions that follow.

were intended primarily to advance the value of federalism in this context. James Madison himself, for example, believed that even under the original Constitution, there was "not a shadow of right in the general government to intermeddle with religion" and that the "least interference with it would be a most flagrant usurpation."[29] The framers and ratifiers of the Religion Clauses agreed with Madison concerning the impropriety of national involvement in this area, but they wished to make the point explicit. Thus, directing themselves explicitly to *Congress*, they acted to limit the scope of national power and to preserve the power of the states to address religion and religious liberty as the states saw fit.

Especially on the issue of disestablishment, the states, as a matter of general principle, in fact reflected divergent views at the time of the First Amendment's adoption. The Virginia understanding was far from universal. Seven states, including Virginia, had adopted a policy of disestablishment. The remaining six states, however, continued to maintain or authorize established religions.[30] Given this widespread and deep division, Congress and the

29. 3 The Debates in the Several State Conventions on the Adoption of the Federal Constitution 330 (Jonathan Elliot ed., 2d ed. 1836) (quoting Madison during the Virginia ratification debates, June 12, 1788), *reprinted in* 5 The Founders' Constitution, *supra* note 6, at 88.

30. For a detailed account of the policies that prevailed in the various states, see Leonard W. Levy, The Establishment Clause: Religion and the First Amendment 25–62 (1986).

ratifying state legislatures plainly could not have agreed on a statement of general principles concerning religious liberty and the proper relationship between religion and government. Had the First Amendment been thought to adopt such a statement, it would not have been enacted. The framers and ratifiers could and did agree, however, that there should be no *national* church or other *national* establishment of religion, and, more generally, they agreed that *Congress* was not to legislate on the subject of religion. This purpose honored the disestablishment policies of states like Virginia, but it also preserved the establishments that existed elsewhere as a matter of state law. The appropriate breadth—or at least the appropriate phrasing—of the Religion Clauses was a matter that received considerable attention in the First Congress, but primarily as an issue concerning the appropriate means for effecting a policy of federalism on questions of church and state. Indeed, the final language of the Establishment Clause—"Congress shall make no law *respecting* an establishment of religion"— seems well-suited not only to preclude congressional establishments, but also to protect the existing state establishments from congressional interference.

As applied to congressional action, the original understanding of the Religion Clauses is genuinely debatable. This debate, however, should be viewed through the lens of federalism. The stronger the framers' and ratifiers' embrace of federalism in this area, the broader their intended prohibition on

Congress. As to the Establishment Clause, if the framers and ratifiers intended only a limited prohibition on discriminatory favoritism, as Chief Justice Rehnquist contended, it was because they were satisfied that this would resolve their federalism concerns. If they intended a broader prohibition on generalized support for religion, as the Supreme Court has declared, it was because they supported an even stronger policy of federalism, one that would remove from Congress and preserve to the states an even broader segment of legislative power. As to the Free Exercise Clause, the original understanding might or might not include exemptions from federal regulations of conduct. This question obviously implicates religious liberty, but it cannot be divorced from the congressional context and the fundamental policy of federalism. Thus, in resolving the exemptions question, the search is for the original understanding of a federalistic prohibition on congressional "intermeddling" or "interference" with religion.[31]

31. This federalistic interpretation of the original understanding of the Religion Clauses is not undisputed, but it remains the most coherent explanation of why the Clauses were adopted. As to the Establishment Clause in particular, compare, for example, Noah Feldman, *The Intellectual Origins of the Establishment Clause*, 77 N.Y.U. L. Rev. 346 (2002) (rejecting the federalistic interpretation and arguing that the Establishment Clause was designed to promote a substantive value, liberty of conscience), with Steven D. Smith, *The Jurisdictional Establishment Clause: A Reappraisal*, 81 Notre Dame L. Rev. 1843 (2006) (systematically rebutting the criticisms and competing arguments of Feldman and others and concluding that the federalistic or "jurisdictional" interpretation is the best and most persuasive account of the original understanding).

The Original Understanding and Fourteenth Amendment "Incorporation"

Despite the justices' protestations, their debates about the original understanding of the Religion Clauses are of limited help and of limited importance. Even as to congressional action and even when informed by the appropriate federalistic perspective, the debates are inconclusive. More important, the bulk of the Court's cases address state, not federal, governmental policies, and the framers and ratifiers of the First Amendment certainly did not intend to impose any limitations on the states. As noted above, the Supreme Court has cited the Fourteenth Amendment as authority for applying the Religion Clauses to the states. To evaluate this claim of "incorporation" as a matter of originalist inquiry, of course, we must consider the original understanding not of the First Amendment, but of the Fourteenth. Ratified in 1868 during the aftermath of the Civil War, the Fourteenth Amendment includes general language barring the states from "abridg[ing] the privileges or immunities of citizens of the United States" and from "depriv[ing] any person of life, liberty, or property, without due process of law."

The Supreme Court's incorporation doctrine, which has extended most of the Bill of Rights to the states, is as well-settled as constitutional doctrine can be. In terms of the original understanding, however, it is far from clear that the general language of the Fourteenth Amendment was intended to accomplish this far-reaching result. In any event, there is evidence that the framers and ratifiers of the Fourteenth Amendment, whatever their intentions with respect to the Bill of Rights generally, at least did not intend to incorporate the Religion Clauses. In 1875 and 1876, less than ten years after the adoption of the Fourteenth Amendment, Congress carefully considered, but eventually rejected, a proposed constitutional amendment that was specifically designed to make the Religion Clauses applicable to the states. The proposed "Blaine Amendment" would have provided, in part, that "[n]o *State* shall make any law respecting an establishment of religion or prohibiting the free exercise thereof."[32] The Blaine Amendment generated considerable attention and debate in Congress, but no one suggested that the amendment's establishment and free exercise provisions were superfluous—as they would have been, of course, if the Fourteenth Amendment had *already* incorporated the Religion Clauses. Post-ratification congressional action or inaction can be a hazardous basis for determining the original understanding of a constitutional amendment. In this case, however, the post-ratification evidence concerning the Blaine Amendment strongly suggests that the Fourteenth Amendment, as originally understood, did not incorporate the Religion Clauses for application to the states.

32. H.R.J. Res. 1, 44th Cong., 1st Sess., 4 Cong. Rec. 205 (1875) (emphasis added).

More generally, an originalist incorporation of the Religion Clauses is logically problematic, if not impossible. As to incorporation generally, the originalist contention is that the framers and ratifiers of the Fourteenth Amendment intended to incorporate the Bill of Rights by reference, making its principles—as originally understood for application to the federal government—henceforth apply to the states in the same way. To the extent that a Bill of Rights provision, as originally understood, reflected a general principle concerning the proper role of government and the rights of individuals, the framers and ratifiers of the Fourteenth Amendment might logically have concluded that the Constitution should be extended to protect that principle against state as well as federal infringement. As we have seen, however, the Religion Clauses, as originally understood, were not intended to adopt general principles. Instead, they were linked directly to the policy of federalism, and, accordingly, they were specifically designed to limit congressional power and congressional power alone. If, indeed, the Religion Clauses primarily reflect a policy of states' rights, to incorporate the Clauses for application *against* the states is logical non-sense, akin to applying the Tenth Amendment against the states.[33]

33. Justice Thomas recently has adopted this argument in part, contending that the Establishment Clause—but not the Free Exercise Clause—should be understood as "a federalism provision, which, for this reason, resists incorporation." Elk Grove Unified Sch. Dist. v. Newdow, 542 U.S. 1, 45 (2004) (Thomas, J., concurring in the judgment); *see id.* at 49–51.

Theoretically, the framers and ratifiers of the Fourteenth Amendment could have intended to incorporate the Religion Clauses despite the seeming illogic of such action. Thus, even though the Religion Clauses were designed primarily to advance the policy of federalism, their prohibitions against federal action could have been extended to the states for other, non-federalistic reasons. In particular, the framers and ratifiers of the Fourteenth Amendment might have intended to impose on the states, as a matter of general principle, prohibitions that had been formulated for a quite different and more limited purpose—that of restricting federal power and, at the same time, preserving the power of the states. But this certainly would have been an odd and circuitous way to fashion constitutional norms. As a result, we should not readily impute this sort of decisionmaking to the officials who adopted the Fourteenth Amendment.[34]

34. A somewhat different claim is that the framers and ratifiers of the Fourteenth Amendment, by the time that amendment was adopted, had their own understandings of religious free exercise and disestablishment, and that they meant to include them in the Fourteenth Amendment—without regard to the original understanding or original purpose of the First Amendment as such. *See* Kurt T. Lash, *The Second Adoption of the Free Exercise Clause: Religious Exemptions Under the Fourteenth Amendment,* 88 Nw. U. L. Rev. 1106 (1994); Kurt T. Lash, *The Second Adoption of the Establishment Clause: The Rise of the Nonestablishment Principle,* 27 Ariz. St. L.J. 1085 (1995). This claim is logically more plausible than incorporation pure and simple, but the historical evidence supporting this argument is linked to the framers' and ratifiers' special concerns about slave religion and its suppression in the South. It is difficult to infer from this evidence a collective intention to protect more general free exercise and disestablishment values, especially in

Contrary to the Supreme Court's position, the Fourteenth Amendment, as originally understood, probably did not incorporate the Religion Clauses for application to the states. At the very least, the federalistic purpose of the Religion Clauses, and the logical problem that this creates, should place a heavy burden of persuasion on those who contend that the Fourteenth Amendment was intended to have this effect. Given that the originalist argument for incorporating *any* of the Bill of Rights is contentious, and given the circumstances surrounding the Blaine Amendment, it is difficult to imagine how this burden could be met.[35]

light of the Blaine Amendment. In any event, the Supreme Court has not embraced this argument, relying instead on incorporation pure and simple, which leads the Court back to the First Amendment and to arguments invoking Madison and Jefferson.

35. There is an additional, textual reason for doubting that the original understanding of the Fourteenth Amendment can justify an incorporation of the Establishment Clause. The text of the Fourteenth Amendment refers to the protection of "privileges" and "immunities" of "citizens," as well as the rights of "persons" to be free from unlawful "deprivations" of "life, liberty, or property." This language seems ill-suited for incorporating the Establishment Clause, which, at least in part, is a structural provision that is not directly linked to the rights or liberties of specific individuals. *Cf.* Zelman v. Simmons–Harris, 536 U.S. 639, 678–80 (2002) (Thomas, J., concurring) (arguing that the Establishment Clause should be incorporated only if and to the extent that it protects individual religious liberty); *but cf.* School Dist. of Abington Township v. Schempp, 374 U.S. 203, 256–58 (1963) (Brennan, J., concurring) (defending incorporation on the ground that the Establishment Clause, without limitation, should be read along with the Free Exercise Clause as a "coguarantor" of religious liberty).

Conclusion

In summary, the Supreme Court's decisionmaking under the Religion Clauses, as applied to congressional action, can reasonably be debated in originalist terms, although these debates too often ignore the important role of federalism. In any event, the debates are inconclusive. More important, the vast majority of the Court's decisionmaking addresses state, not federal, governmental policies. This decisionmaking rests on a theory of Fourteenth Amendment incorporation that, in originalist terms, is dubious at best. To put it mildly, the original understanding is an overrated source of constitutional values in this area. Although the justices frequently invoke it, their arguments are misleading and unhelpful.[36]

36. No discussion of the Supreme Court's originalist maneuvering is complete without mention of *Marsh v. Chambers*, 463 U.S. 783 (1983). In *Marsh*, the Court upheld the constitutionality of state-sponsored legislative prayer, even though this practice would appear to violate the Court's general Establishment Clause doctrine. In support of its ruling, the Court suggested that the practice of legislative prayer was exceptional. This practice had been specifically approved by the First Congress, the Court reasoned, rendering it immune from constitutional invalidation because such a result could not be defended in originalist terms. As we have seen, however, the Supreme Court's *general doctrine* under the Religion Clauses—at least as applied to the states—cannot be defended in originalist terms. As a result, the Court's reliance on the original understanding in *Marsh*, as the basis for creating an exception to its general doctrine, does nothing but exacerbate the Court's cut-and-paste use of the historical record.

As we conclude this chapter, one point bears emphasis: to say that the original understanding is largely unimportant in this context is not to say that *history* is unimportant. The original understanding depends on the collective intentions of the framers and ratifiers of the First and Fourteenth Amendments, that is, on the values that they placed in the Constitution through the formal process of constitutional amendment. History, as a source of constitutional values, is not so limited. And as we will see in the next chapter, American history, from the founding to the present, reveals a set of embedded and evolving constitutional values that inform the Religion Clauses in helpful and important ways.

Chapter 3

Embedded and Evolving Constitutional Values

As Chapter 2 revealed, originalism cannot explain or justify the Supreme Court's decisionmaking under the Religion Clauses. Despite the Court's claims to the contrary, it has been engaged in a more creative, nonoriginalist process of constitutional interpretation, a process through which the Court has given constitutional effect to values not enacted by the framers and ratifiers of the First Amendment, the Fourteenth Amendment, or any other constitutional provision. And in so doing, the Court has overridden the policy judgments of elected officials, thereby frustrating the ordinary process of majoritarian self-government.

Nonoriginalist constitutional interpretation is controversial, and it exposes the Supreme Court to the charge of judicial activism. Yet in the context of the Religion Clauses, the Court's decisions have not been purely subjective. Rather, they have been based upon broadly shared values—sometimes complementary, sometimes in tension—that have emerged, grown, and evolved over the course of American history. The justices sometimes have disagreed concerning the basic content of the general values that are in play. More often, they have disagreed only about their significance or about their implementation in specific contexts. The Court's nonoriginalist decisionmaking mediates past and present. More art than science, it taps values that are deeply embedded in our political and cultural history, tracks their development over time, and determines their significance for contemporary societal issues. For better or for worse, the Court is not merely a passive interpreter. It is an active and creative interpreter, and its decisions themselves contribute to the evolving content of constitutional values, laying the groundwork for future decisions and continuing constitutional change.

The Supreme Court's nonoriginalist decisionmaking, although not a product of the original understanding, certainly is not ahistorical. To the contrary, it proceeds from and contributes to the continuing history of American religious liberty. We turn next to that history and to the values that it reflects.

A Brief History of American Religious Liberty[1]

As discussed in Chapter 2, the original understanding of the Religion Clauses is much more a

1. Portions of this section draw upon Daniel O. Conkle, *The Path of American Religious Liberty: From the Original Theology to Formal Neutrality and an Uncertain Future*, 75 Ind. L.J. 1 (2000).

statement about federalism than it is a statement about the substance of religious liberty. Even so, the substantive idea of religious liberty was firmly planted in the founding period—in Virginia and elsewhere. There was deep disagreement on basic issues, including especially the issue of disestablishment. As noted earlier, this precluded an agreement on substance when the Religion Clauses were enacted. Despite the differences among the various states, however, all of them, to one degree or another, embraced the general idea of religious liberty.

For the Founders,[2] the substantive idea of religious liberty—whatever its precise boundaries—was rooted not in secular philosophy, but in theology. Thus, the central justification for religious liberty was distinctly religious, resting on the combination of two theological principles: first, that religious duties are more important than secular duties, and second, that individuals must undertake their religious duties voluntarily, not under legal compulsion.[3] The Virginia experience is notable. Thus, in his *Memorial and Remonstrance Against Religious Assessments*, James Madison noted that "[i]t is the duty of every man to render to the Creator such

2. Freed from the constraints of originalist inquiry, the discussion here is not about the framers and ratifiers of the First Amendment, but about the Founders generally, describing their dominant arguments and understandings.

3. *See* Steven D. Smith, *The Rise and Fall of Religious Freedom in Constitutional Discourse*, 140 U. Pa. L. Rev. 149, 154–66 (1991).

homage and such only as he believes to be acceptable to him. This duty is precedent, both in order of
time and in degree of obligation, to the claims of
Civil Society."[4] To the same effect, Thomas Jefferson's Virginia Act for Religious Freedom declares
that "Almighty God hath created the mind free"
and that compelled religion is "a departure from
the plan of the Holy Author of our religion, who,
being Lord both of body and mind, yet chose not to
propagate it by coercions on either, as was in his
Almighty power to do."[5]

The Founders' religious justification for religious
liberty, complete with its emphasis on religious
voluntarism, was grounded in (Protestant) Christian thought. More generally, Christian values and
insights were intrinsically connected to the political
culture of the new nation. There was rhetoric of
religious equality, but it was designed mainly to
protect the equality of competing Christian denominations. As between Christian and non-Christian
religions, the Founders clearly presupposed the primacy of Christianity. They understood that at least
at the state level, Christianity was entitled to political and legal support as the favored, if not established, religion.

Even the new federal government, despite the
Religion Clauses, offered certain forms of support

4.   James Madison, Memorial and Remonstrance Against Religious Assessments (June 20, 1785), *reprinted in* 5 The Founders'
Constitution 82, 82 (Philip B. Kurland & Ralph Lerner eds.,
1987).

5.   Virginia Act for Religious Freedom, Va. Code Ann. § 57–1
(2008) (enacted Jan. 16, 1786).

for Christianity. Federal facilities in all three branches, including the hall of the House of Representatives, were routinely used for Sunday worship services. As president, Thomas Jefferson regularly attended Sunday services in the House, where, with Jefferson's tacit approval, the Marine Band provided accompaniment for the hymns. Notably, President Jefferson began his attendance the first Sunday after he sent his famous letter to the Danbury Baptists, lauding the Religion Clauses and declaring that they had created a "wall of separation" between church and state![6]

Justice Joseph Story captured the general sentiment of the Founders: "that Christianity ought to receive encouragement from the state, so far as was not incompatible with the private rights of conscience, and the freedom of religious worship. An attempt to level all religions ... would have created universal disapprobation, if not universal indignation."[7] Justice Story was describing the founding period, but a similar understanding prevailed throughout the nineteenth century and well into the twentieth. To be sure, the states with formal religious establishments dissolved them in the early decades of the new nation, thereby moving, in that respect, to adopt the Virginia understanding for themselves. The last formal establish-

6. *See* James H. Hutson, Religion and the Founding of the American Republic 84–94 (1998).

7. 3 Joseph Story, Commentaries on the Constitution § 1868 (1833), *reprinted in* 5 The Founders' Constitution, *supra* note 4, at 108, 109.

ment was dissolved by Massachusetts in 1833.[8] Formal disestablishment achieved an important measure of institutional separation between church and state, protecting the jurisdictional domain of each from improper intrusion by the other. Formal disestablishment, however, certainly did not mean the end of primacy and legal favoritism for Christianity. In 1892, for example, based on its survey of American law and culture, the Supreme Court declared that "this is a Christian nation."[9] And some forty years later, in 1931, the Court officially reaffirmed that "[w]e are a Christian people."[10]

This sort of language soon disappeared from judicial opinions, however, and there was in the twentieth century a gradual but dramatic shift of thinking. Driven by changing religious demographics and evolving values, the American understanding of religious liberty eventually rejected the idea of legally sanctioned Christian dominance, embracing instead a vigorous requirement of equality between and among all religions. Thus, in the latter half of the twentieth century, the Supreme Court interpreted the Religion Clauses to preclude the government from favoring Christianity—for example, through the sponsorship of Christian prayers in the public schools. Under civil rights legislation enacted by Congress in the 1960s, moreover, even non-govern-

8. Leonard W. Levy, The Establishment Clause: Religion and the First Amendment 38 (1986).

9. Church of the Holy Trinity v. United States, 143 U.S. 457, 471 (1892).

10. United States v. Macintosh, 283 U.S. 605, 625 (1931).

mental religious discrimination was forbidden in public accommodations, employment, and housing. Clearly, the legal culture, and with it the public culture, was shifting decidedly from Christian dominance to religious equality.

This trend has continued, and today religious equality is a central and uncontested constitutional value. The Supreme Court has renounced the Christian dominance that prevailed in the past, and it has interpreted the Religion Clauses to reflect a strong constitutional commitment to equal treatment for all religions, Christian and non-Christian alike. Even the Court's critics have applauded this "no preference" requirement. Chief Justice Rehnquist, for example, despite his fundamental disagreement with other aspects of the Court's doctrine, agreed that the government was precluded "from asserting a preference for one religious denomination or sect over others."[11] As we will see in later chapters, the value of religious equality plays a powerful role in contemporary constitutional interpretation, strongly influencing the Court's decision-making under both the Free Exercise Clause and the Establishment Clause.

More controversially, the law has increasingly extended the idea of religious equality to mean equality not only among religions, but also between religion and irreligion. According to this view, the government cannot disfavor religion in general, but neither can the government favor or support it, for

11. Wallace v. Jaffree, 472 U.S. 38, 113 (1985) (Rehnquist, J., dissenting).

example, by sponsoring a nondenominational prayer or a general religious statement or display. A far cry from the Founders' preferential treatment of religion in general and Christianity in particular, the idea of equal treatment for religion and irreligion is largely a product of the modern era. It reflects the ever-increasing importance of equality as a basic value in the United States. It also reflects the secularization of public life, the growth of new and unusual forms of religion, and a diminished ability to distinguish what is "religious" from what is not. Although some justices have strongly objected, the Supreme Court generally has embraced the idea of equal treatment between religion and irreligion, and, along with the requirement of equal treatment among religions, it has become a dominant theme in contemporary doctrine. This theme disfavors special or discriminatory treatment of religion, whether for its benefit or to its disadvantage. Thus, under the Free Exercise Clause, the Court generally has rejected claims that religious conduct should be granted special exemptions from nondiscriminatory laws, and, under the Establishment Clause, the Court has been inclined to permit the nondiscriminatory inclusion of religious beneficiaries in general funding programs.

At the founding, America was almost exclusively Christian and was overwhelmingly Protestant. Today, although Christianity still predominates, American religion is remarkably and increasingly pluralistic, and nonbelief is viewed by many as a legitimate personal stance. In response to the religious pluralism and diversity of contemporary America, the Supreme Court's recent emphasis on religious equality sometimes has included special sensitivity to the interests of religious minorities and nonbelievers. For example, the Court has broadly expanded an individual's "freedom to choose his own creed" and "his right to refrain from accepting the creed established by the majority":

At one time it was thought that this right merely proscribed the preference of one Christian sect over another, but would not require equal respect for the conscience of the infidel, the atheist, or the adherent of a non-Christian faith such as Islam or Judaism. But when the underlying principle has been examined in the crucible of litigation, the Court has unambiguously concluded that the individual freedom of conscience protected by the First Amendment embraces the right to select any religious faith or none at all.[12]

In its interpretations of the Establishment Clause, the Supreme Court has gone even further, stating that the government cannot endorse a majority faith, or religion in general, because of the affront and offense that the government's message might inflict upon religious minorities and nonbelievers. The Court's concern about endorsement and affront is designed to protect not only the consciences of dissenting citizens, but also their religious identities and personal self-understandings. In addition, it is intended to promote the mainte-

12. *Id.* at 52–53 (majority opinion) (footnotes omitted).

nance of a religiously inclusive political community. According to an influential opinion by Justice O'Connor, governmental endorsement of religion "sends a message to nonadherents that they are outsiders, not full members of the political community, and an accompanying message to adherents that they are insiders, favored members of the political community."[13] The Establishment Clause forbids such messages, she wrote, because it "prohibits government from making adherence to a religion relevant in any way to a person's standing in the political community."[14] Although the Founders would surely have disagreed, this reasoning supports the view that governmental endorsement of religion, however generic, is constitutionally unacceptable in the contemporary United States.

As this brief historical survey suggests, the Founders started America on the path of religious liberty, but they did not chart our ultimate destination. Over the past two centuries, old values have been sometimes reaffirmed and sometimes transformed as more modern values and new circumstances have risen to prominence. The contemporary Supreme Court claims an originalist pedigree for its decisionmaking under the Religion Clauses. In reality, the Court has played a far more creative role, drawing upon a complex and interrelated set of evolving constitutional values.

13. Lynch v. Donnelly, 465 U.S. 668, 688 (1984) (O'Connor, J., concurring).

14. *Id.* at 687.

Contemporary Constitutional Values

In the contemporary period, the Religion Clauses can be understood to protect at least six values or groups of values. The first three attend primarily to the rights and interests of individuals. The next two focus on broader political and religious interests. The final value is specifically linked to American tradition. These various values sometimes work in harmony, but are sometimes in conflict.

Religious Voluntarism

In its most basic sense, religious "liberty" means religious voluntarism, that is, the freedom to make religious choices for oneself, free from governmental compulsion or improper influence. The value of religious voluntarism emerged in the founding period, supported by the Founders' religious justification for religious liberty. The contours of this value have evolved over time, influenced by the growing importance of religious equality and by an increased sensitivity to the interests of religious minorities and nonbelievers. Today, the value of religious voluntarism promotes the right to choose any religion or none at all, and it guards not only against governmental compulsion or coercion, but also against more subtle forms of governmental influence. Standing alone and given vigorous protection, this value would require that government "minimize the extent to which it either encourages or discourages religious belief or disbelief, practice or nonpractice, observance or nonobservance," leaving religion "as wholly to private choice as anything can be."[15]

Respecting Religious Identity

An individual's religious identity—whether it affirms a particular religion or rejects religion altogether—often is central to his or her self-understanding. Religious voluntarism protects religious choices, including the choice of rejecting religion. Yet the government might cause religion-related injuries, albeit intangible, even when its actions do not affect religious choices and therefore do not impair the value of religious voluntarism. If the government fails to respect the religious identity of one of its citizens, the government's action, even if purely symbolic, may assault the person's sense of self, causing offense, affront, and alienation. The contemporary Supreme Court has been sensitive to this concern, and it has afforded constitutional protection to the value that it implicates—respecting the religious identity of citizens. This value has played an important role, for example, in Establishment Clause decisions prohibiting the government from endorsing religion even when there is little risk that the government's endorsement will meaningfully influence religious choices. As suggested earlier, this prohibition can be linked to the protection of dissenters—typically, religious minorities and nonbelievers—whose religious identity and sense of self can be threatened when the govern-

15. Douglas Laycock, *Formal, Substantive, and Disaggregated Neutrality Toward Religion*, 39 DePaul L. Rev. 993, 1001–02 (1990).

ment endorses religious beliefs the dissenters do not share, sending a message that the dissenters are "outsiders, not full members of the political community."

Religious Equality: "Substantive Equality" and "Formal Equality"

In recent decades, religious equality has grown to become a dominant value under the Religion Clauses. Indeed, it may now be the most important value of all, at least in the eyes of the contemporary Supreme Court. Religious equality today includes not only equality between and among religions, Christian and non-Christian alike, but also between religion and irreligion. It means that the government cannot take action that prefers or disfavors Christianity or Christians, as opposed to other religions or religious believers, nor can it act to advantage or disadvantage religion or religious individuals in general, as opposed to nonbelief or nonbelievers.

This general description of religious equality, also known as religious neutrality, leaves open the question of precisely how this value should be understood and implemented. "Substantive equality" or "substantive neutrality" calls for governmental action that has an equal *impact* on citizens of all religions or of no religion, even if this requires the government to take religion into account in certain contexts. The equal-impact model might work hand in hand with the value of religious voluntarism by seeking to minimize the government's promotion or discouragement of religious choices and conduct, attaining an *equal* impact that is also a *minimal* impact. "Formal equality" or "formal neutrality," by contrast, looks not to the impact but to the form or intent of the government's action. It precludes formal or deliberate discrimination either between or among religions or between religion and irreligion. Analogous to the Fourteenth Amendment's Equal Protection Clause prohibition on purposeful discrimination based on race,[16] formal equality in the context of religion would prohibit the government from taking religion into account by forbidding "classification in terms of religion either to confer a benefit or to impose a burden."[17] As later chapters will show, the contemporary Supreme Court has increasingly utilized the formal model of equality, a model that sometimes complements other constitutional values, including religious voluntarism, but that sometimes conflicts with them.

Political Values: Promoting a Religiously Inclusive Political Community and Protecting Government from Improper Religious Involvement

The Religion Clauses, including especially the Establishment Clause, can be seen to serve institu-

---

16. *See, e.g.*, Washington v. Davis, 426 U.S. 229 (1976); Village of Arlington Heights v. Metropolitan Housing Development Corp., 429 U.S. 252 (1977); Hunter v. Underwood, 471 U.S. 222 (1985). The Supreme Court itself has invoked this analogy in the Free Exercise context, citing *Washington v. Davis* as a relevant precedent. *See* Employment Div. v. Smith, 494 U.S. 872, 886 n.3 (1990).

17. Philip B. Kurland, *Of Church and State and the Supreme Court*, 29 U. Chi. L. Rev. 1, 96 (1961). *See* Laycock, *supra* note 15, at 999. The distinction between "substantive" and "formal" equality or neutrality is drawn from Professor Laycock's article, although Laycock would further distinguish "equality" from "neutrality."

tional or structural values in addition to values linked more directly to the rights and interests of individuals. In particular, the Establishment Clause can be understood to serve political values, protecting the government and the political community from certain forms of religious involvement. Historically, governments with formal religious establishments "had incurred the hatred, disrespect and even contempt of those who held contrary beliefs," tending " 'to enervate the laws in general, and to slacken the bands of Society.' "[18] More broadly, the Supreme Court has suggested that inherently religious issues should not be decided by governmental mechanisms, including majoritarian voting, because "[s]uch a system encourages divisiveness along religious lines."[19] Furthermore, under the reasoning of Justice O'Connor, even the mere governmental endorsement of religion is understood to affront and alienate dissenting citizens, relegating them to "outsider" status and thereby weakening the political community itself. In these respects, the contemporary Establishment Clause is promoting a political value, the maintenance of a religiously inclusive political community.

18. Engel v. Vitale, 370 U.S. 421, 431 & n.13 (1962) (quoting James Madison, Memorial and Remonstrance Against Religious Assessments (June 20, 1785), *reprinted in* 5 The Founders' Constitution, *supra* note 4, at 82, 84).

19. Santa Fe Indep. Sch. Dist. v. Doe, 530 U.S. 290, 317 (2000).

In its decisions promoting a religiously inclusive political community, the Supreme Court typically has focused on governmental action addressing matters that are inherently and indisputably religious, such as the government's promotion of prayer or its endorsement of particular understandings of God. Some have contended that the Court's concern should also extend to governmental policymaking on nonspiritual, worldly issues—for example, issues relating to abortion, the death penalty, welfare, or environmental protection—when such issues are decided on the basis of moral values that are religious in derivation. They argue that even in the context of worldly issues, religious politics can be divisive and can be "undemocratic" to the extent that the religious viewpoints are closed-minded or are "inaccessible" to other citizens. Others reject this position, noting that religiously informed moral values have played an important political role throughout American history. They contend that to restrict this role would impair the political equality of religious citizens, and they claim that religiously informed moral arguments are not invariably more closed-minded or inaccessible than secular ones. The Supreme Court's position is not entirely clear. Although the Court has declared that lawmaking must be supported by a "secular" purpose, it has never used this requirement to invalidate a law addressing a matter that is not inherently religious. Even so, there are continuing suggestions that the contemporary Establishment Clause may or should protect the government from the influence of religion, even in the context of worldly issues.

Religious Values: Protecting Religion from Government and Protecting the Autonomy of Religious Institutions

In addition to political values, the Religion Clauses also serve religious values that likewise are institutional or structural in nature: protecting religion as such and protecting the autonomy of religious institutions. The Founders believed that religion was valuable and important, both intrinsically and for the maintenance of the American society and political system. They believed that government should encourage religion to a degree, but they also believed that government should neither coerce religion nor tarnish or corrupt it for secular purposes, allowing religion to thrive in the private domain and in the hands of religious institutions. Often associated with Roger Williams, the leader of colonial Rhode Island, this view supported not only the free exercise of religion, but also the historical trend toward disestablishment. James Madison, for example, argued in his *Memorial and Remonstrance* that the establishment of religion actually harmed religion and that for the government to "employ Religion as an engine of Civil policy" was "an unhallowed perversion of the means of salvation."[20]

These sorts of arguments, supporting a separation of church and state for the protection of reli-

20. James Madison, Memorial and Remonstrance Against Religious Assessments (June 20, 1785), *reprinted in* 5 The Founders' Constitution, *supra* note 4, at 82, 83.

gious values, are somewhat less common today, but they have continuing force in contemporary America. Most Americans continue to believe that religion is valuable and important, and they believe that religious institutions play an important role in American society. At the same time, many would contend that in today's cultural climate, governmental "support" for religion, even short of formal establishment, runs the risk of degrading and weakening religion and of compromising the independence and integrity of religious institutions. The government might attempt to promote religion symbolically, perhaps through the sponsorship of prayer or religious displays. In recognition of our religious diversity, however, this type of symbolic action today is likely to invoke a broadly inclusive or generic religion—in effect, a "lowest common denominator" religion—that might tend to undermine, not support, the special and sacred character of genuine religion. In the alternative, the government might attempt to provide more tangible support for religion, directly or indirectly, perhaps by including religious schools or other religious institutions in more general funding programs. But governmental funding programs typically include conditions that participants must honor, conditions that may expand over time even as the participants become more and more dependent on the government's financial support. These sorts of conditions can threaten the autonomy of religious institutions, inducing them to modify and weaken their religious practices and requirements in response to the government's demands.

These arguments suggest that religious values—protecting religion and its maintenance and nurture by autonomous religious institutions—may support not only the free exercise of religion, but at least some degree of separation between church and state. If so, the religious values may often work in tandem with other constitutional values, including religious voluntarism as well as the political values of promoting an inclusive political community and protecting government from improper religious involvement. They may sometimes be in conflict with other values, however, including the value of religious equality, at least when religious equality is understood in terms of formal equality, which disfavors special protection or special treatment for religion or religious institutions.

Preserving Traditional Governmental Practices

Some justices, including especially Justice Scalia, have argued that tradition should be a basic touchstone of constitutional interpretation. In its interpretations of the Religion Clauses, the contemporary Supreme Court has not followed this approach. Indeed, some of the Court's Establishment Clause doctrine, requiring a secular purpose for lawmaking and precluding the government from endorsing religion, is inconsistent with the traditional understanding—dating back to the founding—that the government should (to some degree) promote and encourage religion. Even so, the Court does not ignore tradition, which acts as something of a wild card in its Establishment Clause decisionmaking. The practice of legislative prayer by a paid legislative chaplain, for example, might seem a quintessential violation of the Establishment Clause, but the Court has upheld it in a decision emphasizing that legislative prayer is such a longstanding American tradition that it is "part of the fabric of our society."[21] Tradition might also explain the constitutionality of certain other governmental practices that endorse religion, including our national motto, "In God We Trust." In cases such as these, the value of preserving traditional governmental practices acts as a counterweight to other constitutional values that might suggest a constitutional violation. The precise weight of tradition, relative to other values, is not entirely clear, but it tends to support the constitutionality of governmental endorsements of religion that are deeply traditional, nonsectarian, symbolic (as opposed to financially substantial), and non-coercive.

Constitutional Values and Constitutional Interpretation

This chapter has outlined the history of American religious liberty and has explained how, over the

21. Marsh v. Chambers, 463 U.S. 783, 792 (1983). As discussed in the final footnote of Chapter 2, the Court also observed that the practice of legislative prayer had been specifically approved by the First Congress and therefore could not be said to violate the original understanding of the First Amendment.

course of that history, the Supreme Court has drawn upon and contributed to an evolving set of constitutional values. These values are the primary source for the Court's interpretations of the Religion Clauses, but the guidance that they provide is insufficient to dictate particular decisions or particular formulations of constitutional doctrine. Taken individually, the various values are sufficiently vague and general that their implications are not always clear. Taken together, they may point in different directions. The Court's interpretations of the Religion Clauses therefore depend not only on these values, but also on the Court's evaluation of these values and their implications, both individually and collectively. This evaluation is reflected in the Court's doctrinal formulations as well as its particular decisions. We turn next to a systematic examination of the Court's interpretations of the Religion Clauses, beginning with doctrinal fundamentals.

CHAPTER 4

INTERPRETING THE RELIGION CLAUSES: DOCTRINAL FUNDAMENTALS

The Supreme Court's doctrine under the Religion Clauses is complex and multifaceted. The Court has separate doctrinal tests and approaches for the Free Exercise and Establishment Clauses, and its decisions, especially under the Establishment Clause, can be further divided into a number of doctrinal categories. Before examining the Court's doctrine in all its fullness, however, it is important to begin with doctrinal fundamentals, that is, with general concepts and principles that are basic to the Religion Clauses generally. Thus, we will examine the concepts of impermissible burdens and impermissible benefits, the general principle of nondiscrimination, the definition of "religion," and judicial inquiries into the content and sincerity of religious beliefs. These fundamentals will serve as building blocks for understanding the Court's more specific doctrine and decisions.

Impermissible Burdens and Impermissible Benefits

At the broadest level, the Supreme Court reads the Religion Clauses, taken together, to promote a general policy of governmental neutrality or even-handedness toward religion. In so doing, however, the Court treats the Free Exercise and Establishment Clauses as distinct, albeit related, provisions. The Free Exercise Clause prohibits the government from mistreating religion through the imposition of impermissible burdens. Conversely, the Establishment Clause forbids the government from advantaging religion through the conferral of impermissible benefits.

What counts as "impermissible" under either clause is a critical and often difficult question. But even the question of what counts as a "burden" or a "benefit" can be troublesome, and, given the differing implications of the two clauses, this question also can be quite important. Suppose, for example, that a law makes it a crime to use peyote, an hallucinogenic drug, but that the law includes an exception for the religious use of peyote, which is commonly consumed for sacramental purposes by members of the Native American Church. The religious exemption removes what would otherwise be a legal burden on religion—a criminal penalty—and it therefore could be seen to conform to the Free Exercise Clause. Conversely, this exemption from an otherwise general law arguably confers a special benefit on religion, or perhaps on the particular religion of the Native American Church, thereby raising an issue under the Establishment Clause. As this example suggests, the burden-versus-benefit issue creates a potential tension between the two clauses, a tension to which we will return later.

Impermissible   Burdens: Basic   Free   Exercise Doctrine

For now, however, let us put aside the burden-versus-benefit issue and assume the presence of what is properly regarded as a burden on religion, potentially implicating the Free Exercise Clause. What sorts of burdens are constitutionally imper-missible? We will explore the Supreme Court's Free Exercise doctrine in the next chapter, but it is helpful at this point to highlight the Court's general stance on two basic issues.

First, there is a broad consensus on the Court that, at a minimum, the Free Exercise Clause pro-hibits discriminatory burdens. More precisely, the Clause forbids the government from imposing a substantial legal burden in a manner that discrimi-nates either against religion in general or against any particular religion—at least if the discrimina-tion amounts to formal or deliberate discrimination. Thus, the government cannot target religion for substantial burdens that are not imposed more gen-erally. For example, it clearly would violate the Free Exercise Clause for the government to forbid the use of peyote only when the use is religious or only when the use occurs as part of a Native American Church religious ritual. This constitutional prohibi-tion on discriminatory burdens is presumptive, not absolute, but such burdens trigger an extremely demanding test of strict scrutiny, a test that the government can rarely if ever satisfy.

Second, there is considerably more debate, and there are changing judicial perspectives over time, concerning the question of whether the Free Exercise Clause prohibits substantial burdens on religion that are not discriminatory, or at least not discriminatory in the obvious sense of formal or deliberate discrimination. For example, if a general and nondiscriminatory prohibition on the use of peyote is applied to its sacramental use, is the religious use protected by the Free Exercise Clause? The Court sometimes has suggested that the Free Exercise Clause is implicated in this context and that it might provide protection under a case-by-case evaluation, effectively requiring religion-based exemptions from some nondiscriminatory laws. More recently, the Court has broadly rejected this idea. But as we will see later, the Court's doctrine on this point is contested, and its precise scope is uncertain.

Impermissible Benefits: Basic Establishment Clause Doctrine

The Supreme Court's doctrine of impermissible benefits under the Establishment Clause, the topic of Chapter 6, is quite complex. But it, too, reflects a distinction between discriminatory and nondiscriminatory laws, albeit with various complications. Three broad points are worth noting.

First, the Establishment Clause, as interpreted by the Supreme Court, strongly disfavors discriminatory benefits. Thus, the Clause generally forbids the government from conferring benefits in a manner that discriminates either in favor of religion in general or in favor of any particular religion—again, at least if the discrimination amounts to formal or deliberate discrimination. For example, it violates the Establishment Clause for a public school to sponsor or promote classroom prayer, whether non-sectarian or Christian. A school that engages in this practice is targeting religion or Christianity for a special benefit. The selective favoritism amounts to deliberate discrimination, preferring religion over irreligion or Christianity over other faiths. Like-wise, it clearly would violate the Establishment Clause for the government to fund private religious schools but not secular ones, or to fund only those private schools that are Roman Catholic.

Second, the Court's Establishment Clause doc-trine is especially averse to what might be called sectarian discrimination, that is, governmental ac-tion that discriminates in favor of one or more particular religions, such as Christianity, as opposed to others. There is a broad consensus that sectarian discrimination is presumptively unconstitutional, and, in fact, this prohibition appears to be categori-cal, as the Court has yet to recognize an exception. By contrast, some justices have protested the gener-al Establishment Clause prohibition on nonsectari-an discrimination, that is, discrimination that fa-vors religion over irreligion but that does not favor any particular religion over others. Likewise, some of the Court's decisions suggest that there might be occasional exceptions to the prohibition on nonsec-tarian discrimination, for example, to permit the validation of traditional governmental practices such as our national motto, "In God We Trust."

Third, there is debate and uncertainty, and there are changing judicial perspectives over time, concerning the question of whether the Establishment Clause forbids the conferral of benefits on religion that are not discriminatory, or at least not discriminatory in the sense of formal or deliberate discrimination. For example, if a legislature adopts a general and nondiscriminatory funding program that includes all private schools, does the Establishment Clause nonetheless prevent the extension of this funding to private religious schools? The Court has determined that the Establishment Clause does impose some limits even on nondiscriminatory benefits. Recent cases have suggested that these limits are few, or at least fewer than previously believed, but the Court is deeply divided in this area, and its doctrine remains unsettled.

The General Principle of Nondiscrimination

As our discussion of impermissible burdens and benefits suggests, a general principle of nondiscrimination, disfavoring formal or deliberate discrimination on the basis of religion, is common ground under the Free Exercise and Establishment Clauses. Thus, the Supreme Court's doctrine recognizes—not as an absolute rule but as a general proposition—that the Religion Clauses mean "that government [usually] cannot utilize religion as a standard for action or inaction because these clauses, read together as they should be, [usually] prohibit classification in terms of religion either to confer a benefit or to impose a burden."[1] The principle of nondiscrimination thus encompasses the Court's general disfavoring of discriminatory burdens and discriminatory benefits. Indeed, the Court's reliance on this principle sometimes collapses the distinction between burdens and benefits and gives the Religion Clauses a single and unitary meaning.

The merger of Free Exercise and Establishment Clause doctrine is especially evident in the context of sectarian discrimination. For example, in *Church of the Lukumi Babalu Aye, Inc. v. City of Hialeah*,[2] a case to which we will return in the next chapter, the Court relied on the Free Exercise Clause to invalidate a set of city ordinances that selectively outlawed the Santeria practice of animal sacrifice. The ordinances were carefully crafted to leave other animal killings unaffected—including not only secular killings, but also the Orthodox Jewish practice of Kosher slaughter. According to the Court, the city had deliberately discriminated not so much against religion in general as against the particular religion of Santeria, thereby effecting a type of sectarian discrimination. In *Larson v. Valente*,[3] by

1. Philip B. Kurland, *Of Church and State and the Supreme Court*, 29 U. Chi. L. Rev. 1, 96 (1961). Professor Kurland urged this principle—without the softening of the bracketed qualifiers inserted here—as something much closer to an absolute rule.

2. 508 U.S. 520 (1993).

3. 456 U.S. 228 (1982).

contrast, the Court invoked the Establishment Clause as the basis for invalidating a Minnesota law that exempted religious organizations from certain reporting requirements only if they received no more than half of their contributions from non-members. The Court found that the selective exemption was designed to prefer mainstream and long-standing religions, which generally rely on member contributions, over the unorthodox and unfamiliar religions that do not, including the sometimes controversial Unification Church. As in *Lukumi*, the Court found sectarian discrimination between or among religions and therefore an impermissible "religious gerrymander."

Although the Court in *Larson* emphasized that the challenged law selectively benefitted mainstream religions, it also noted that the law selectively burdened the disadvantaged religions that were required to report. Likewise, if the Court in *Lukumi* had followed the reasoning of *Larson*, it perhaps could have found not only an impermissible burden on Santeria, but also an impermissible benefit for other religions, or at least for Orthodox Judaism. And yet *Lukumi* rested exclusively on the Free Exercise Clause, and *Larson* entirely on the Establishment Clause. Perhaps this makes sense and perhaps not, but in the end it does not particularly matter. When sectarian discrimination is present, the two clauses have virtually the same meaning, rendering the benefit-versus-burden question—and therefore the question of which clause to apply—of little if any doctrinal consequence.

Under each clause, a finding of sectarian discrimination triggers an extremely rigorous test of strict scrutiny. Indeed, the test is so strong that sectarian discrimination probably can never be justified. As the Court declared in *Larson*, sectarian discrimination violates "[t]he clearest command of the Establishment Clause."[4] The contemporary Court apparently is unanimous on this point, which is accepted even by justices who do not join the Court's disapproval of more generalized, nonsectarian discrimination favoring religion in general.[5] By all indications, moreover, the clearest command of the Establishment Clause is also the clearest command of the Free Exercise Clause. To the extent that sectarian discrimination is at work, the general principle of nondiscrimination is very close to an absolute rule.

With respect to nonsectarian discrimination, by contrast, the Court's doctrine under the Free Exercise and Establishment Clauses is neither unitary nor categorical. As we will see in later chapters, the government sometimes is permitted—and, indeed, it sometimes is required—to discriminate between religion and irreligion. In certain contexts, this discrimination might be said to fa-

4. *Id.* at 244.

5. *See, e.g.,* Wallace v. Jaffree, 472 U.S. 38, 113 (1985) (Rehnquist, J., dissenting) (agreeing that the government is precluded "from asserting a preference for one religious denomination or sect over others"); Lee v. Weisman, 505 U.S. 577, 641 (1992) (Scalia, J., dissenting) (agreeing that the Establishment Clause "rule[s] out of order government-sponsored endorsement of religion . . . where the endorsement is sectarian").

vor religion. For example, the government is permitted to deliberately favor religion through certain traditional governmental practices, including legislative prayer. Likewise, as long as it avoids sectarian discrimination of the sort at issue in *Larson*, it sometimes can discriminate in favor of religious organizations by granting them—but not nonreligious organizations—exemptions from employment regulations and other regulatory requirements. In other contexts, the discrimination might be seen to disadvantage religion. For instance, there are Establishment Clause limitations on the flow of governmental financial support to religion and to religious organizations. These limitations effectively require religion-based exclusions from otherwise general programs of funding, exclusions that discriminate on the basis of religion. And the government has some discretion to impose additional religion-based funding exclusions, even beyond those that the Establishment Clause demands.

Although not a categorical rule in every context, the general principle of nondiscrimination is extremely important. This principle gives particular meaning and doctrinal effect to the constitutional value of religious equality. In dramatic contrast with earlier periods of American history, the Supreme Court today understands this value to include equality not only between and among religions, but also, at least in general, between religion and irreligion. At the same time, the Court understands the value primarily in terms of formal as opposed to substantive equality,[6] and, accordingly, its doctrine implements the value primarily by disfavoring formal or deliberate discrimination on the basis of religion. Thus, although sometimes permitted or even required, the Court tends to view religion-based discrimination as presumptively problematic under both the Free Exercise and the Establishment Clauses, honoring the value of religious equality in the formal sense by reading the principle of nondiscrimination as a general prohibition on formal or deliberate discrimination.

To the extent that the Court's doctrine diverges from the general principle of nondiscrimination, it is serving other constitutional values. Depending on the context, it might be honoring the value of religious equality in the sense of substantive equality, or it might be furthering one or more of the other constitutional values—outlined in Chapter 3—that the Religion Clauses can be read to protect: religious voluntarism; respecting religious identity; promoting a religiously inclusive political community and protecting government from improper religious involvement; protecting religion from government and protecting the autonomy of religious institutions; and preserving traditional governmental practices. But the Court's contemporary doctrine includes relatively few departures from the principle of nondiscrimination. It therefore appears that the Court today gives exceptional

6. On the distinction between substantive and formal equality, see the discussion of religious equality in Chapter 3.

priority to the value of religious equality in a formal sense, an emphasis that sharply diminishes the significance of other values.

Defining "Religion"

The definition of religion is a critical issue under the Religion Clauses. The need for a constitutional definition is present even when the doctrinal test is nondiscrimination. The problem of definition, moreover, takes on added importance and complexity to the extent that the Free Exercise and Establishment Clauses are construed to deviate from the principle of nondiscrimination, permitting or requiring special treatment for religion either in the imposition of burdens or in the conferral of benefits. Remarkably, however, the Supreme Court has never adopted a constitutional definition as such and, indeed, it has offered no more than partial and sometimes conflicting suggestions. Generally speaking, the Court's decisions under the Religion Clauses have involved religion in a conventional and indisputable sense, obviating the need for definitional discussions. But the Court's avoidance of this subject may also reflect, in part, its desire to evade what has become a contentious if not intractable problem.[7]

7. Some of the discussion that follows draws upon Daniel O. Conkle, *The Path of American Religious Liberty: From the Original Theology to Formal Neutrality and an Uncertain Future*, 75 Ind. L.J. 1, 28–32 (2000).

For most of our nation's history, the constitutional definition of religion was not an issue. Thus, for the Founders and for generations that followed, the defining characteristic of religion was easily stated and utterly uncontroversial: it was the performance of duties owed to God. This understanding encompassed not only the various strands of Protestant Christianity, but also other traditional religions, including Catholic Christianity and Judaism. By the latter half of the twentieth century, however, increasing pluralism and changing values had placed the Founders' understanding in question.

In its 1965 decision in *United States v. Seeger*,[8] the Supreme Court confronted this new set of circumstances in its most notable attempt to give a modern definition to religion. The Court's effort occurred in the context of statutory interpretation, but it has potential implications for a constitutional definition. In *Seeger*, the Court addressed a statutory religious-liberty provision that protected religious objectors to military service. In its definition of religion, the statute referred to "an individual's belief in a relation to a Supreme Being involving duties superior to those arising from any human relation, but [not including] essentially political, sociological, or philosophical views or a merely personal moral code."[9] To earlier generations, this definition would have seemed entirely unexceptional. But by 1965, it seemed problematic—so much so that the Court saw fit to rewrite the definition, through creative statutory interpretation, to include any "sincere and meaningful" belief that "occupies

8.   380 U.S. 163 (1965).
9.   *Id.* at 165 (quoting 50 U.S.C. App. § 456(j) (1958)).

a place in the life of its possessor parallel to that filled by the orthodox belief in God of one who clearly qualifies for the exemption." So understood, the definition included the beliefs of a conscientious objector who acknowledged his skepticism concerning the existence of God, but who claimed a "belief in and devotion to goodness and virtue for their own sakes, and a religious faith in a purely ethical creed."[10]

Seeger's expansive, "parallel position" understanding of religion—an understanding that included deeply held moral beliefs that were not theistic—reflected the rapidly changing character of religion in the United States. As the Court observed, American religion was remarkably diverse by the 1960s, and it extended well beyond the traditional confines of Christianity and Judaism. Perhaps more important, modern theology was transforming certain strands of the traditional faiths themselves. The Court noted, for example, that Protestant theologian Paul Tillich had concluded that God should no longer be understood "as a projection 'out there' or beyond the skies but as the ground of our very being." And "if that word [God] has not much meaning for you," Tillich explained, "translate it, and speak of the depths of your life, and the source of your being, of your ultimate concern, of what you take seriously without any reservation."[11]

10. *Seeger*, 380 U.S. at 166.

11. *Id.* at 180, 187 (quoting Paul Tillich, The Shaking of the Foundations 57 (1948)).

These trends in American religion have only accelerated since the 1960s. Thus, the diversity of the American religious experience is ever more extraordinary, and the diversity of thought within the traditional faiths is ever more pronounced. As a result, *Seeger*'s expansive definition of religion, if appropriate for the 1960s, arguably is even more compelling today. But however reflective of contemporary understandings, the *Seeger* definition inevitably blurs the distinction between religion and nonreligion.[12] Indeed, if religion includes "the source of your being, of your ultimate concern, of what you take seriously without any reservation," then religious liberty itself becomes potentially problematic, because a broad range of human thought and activity might very well qualify as religious. For example, the Free Exercise Clause could be read to protect a wide range of morally-based objections to legal burdens, and the Establishment Clause might broadly preclude the government from conferring legal benefits or favor on various moral perspectives or ideas. Especially in an era of pervasive government, religious liberty could potentially become unmanageable.

In light of these difficulties, it is not surprising that the Supreme Court has never adopted the *Seeger* approach as a *constitutional* definition of

12. *Cf.* Welsh v. United States, 398 U.S. 333 (1970) (extending the *Seeger* definition to include a conscientious objector who had stricken the word "religious" from his application and who had declared that his beliefs were not religious in any conventional sense).

religion.[13] In its 1972 decision in *Wisconsin v. Yoder*,[14] for example, the Court ruled that the religious practices of the Amish, which were Biblically based, traditional, and communal, were entitled to constitutional protection under the Free Exercise Clause, but it stated that such protection would not extend to practices that were merely "philosophical and personal," based on a "subjective evaluation and rejection of the contemporary secular values accepted by the majority."[15] In a later Free Exercise case, the Court clarified its discussion in *Yoder* by rejecting any implication that beliefs or practices can never qualify as religious in the absence of communal or institutional support. Thus, in its 1989 ruling in *Frazee v. Illinois Department of Employment Security*,[16] the Court protected an individual's strict observance of the Sunday Sabbath even though the individual's belief was not based upon the tenet or teaching of a church or any other religious body. Even so, the individual in *Frazee* was

13. Prior to *Seeger*, the Court had hinted that it might offer a broad constitutional definition, suggesting that the Religion Clauses would extend to "religions . . . which do not teach what would generally be considered a belief in the existence of God" and offering as examples not only Buddhism and Taoism, but also Ethical Culture and Secular Humanism. Torcaso v. Watkins, 367 U.S. 488, 495 n.11 (1961).

14. 406 U.S. 205 (1972).

15. *Id.* at 216. The Court noted that the philosophical views of Henry David Thoreau, for example, would not qualify as religious. *Id.*; *see also id.* at 215–19. In his separate opinion, Justice Douglas noted and protested the Court's apparent departure from the *Seeger* approach. *See id.* at 247–49 (Douglas, J., dissenting in part).

16. 489 U.S. 829 (1989).

a Christian, and he derived the belief from his own interpretation of the Bible. *Frazee* involved a personal belief, but a belief that was nonetheless religious in a very conventional sense. As a result, *Frazee* provides little support for the much broader approach of *Seeger*.

Taken together, *Yoder* and *Frazee* could be read to suggest that for purposes of the Religion Clauses, religion can be individual, but it must be theistic (or otherwise "religious" in a conventional sense).[17] More recently, however, the Court has hinted— albeit in defining constitutional "liberty" outside the specific setting of the Religion Clauses—that it might yet embrace a more capacious, *Seeger*-like understanding. Thus, in its 1992 decision reaffirming the right to choose abortion, the Court spoke of a constitutionally protected "zone of conscience and belief," "choices central to personal dignity and autonomy," "spiritual imperatives," and "the right to define one's own concept of existence, of meaning, of the universe, and of the mystery of human life."[18] Although written in the context of abortion, this language strongly suggests that the contemporary Court finds constitutional value in decisions of conscience, that is, decisions of moral self-definition and self-determination that might or might not be religious in a conventional sense.

17. Buddhism, for example, is essentially non-theistic. Even under a conventional definition of religion, however, Buddhism presumably would qualify on the basis of its traditional stature as a religion.

18. Planned Parenthood v. Casey, 505 U.S. 833, 851–52 (1992).

The issue of defining religion presents the Supreme Court with a dilemma. A narrow and conventional definition—generally confining religion to theistic beliefs and practices—might be more readily formulated and certainly would permit a more manageable constitutional doctrine. But a much broader definition, along the lines of *Seeger*, might better reflect the evolving values and changing "religious" understandings of the contemporary United States. A partial response to this dilemma is the Court's emphasis on the value of formal equality and on a doctrinal test of nondiscrimination, a test that reduces the significance of the definitional issue. More generally, the Court has managed largely to evade the problem, leaving the issue of definition unsettled and unresolved.

Academic commentators have proposed a variety of solutions, ranging from essentially conventional definitions, to variants of the *Seeger* approach, to reasoning by analogy in a more comprehensive and contextualized fashion, to a dual approach that would use a broad definition for the Free Exercise Clause but a more narrow one for the Establishment Clause.[19] A unitary conventional definition

19. For a sampling of the academic literature, see Jesse H. Choper, *Defining "Religion" in the First Amendment*, 1982 U. Ill. L. Rev. 579 (proposing a definition that would confine religion to concerns about "extemporal consequences," such as life after death); George C. Freeman, III, *The Misguided Search for the Constitutional Definition of "Religion"*, 71 Geo. L.J. 1519 (1983) (proposing an analogical approach); Kent Greenawalt, *Religion as a Concept in Constitutional Law*, 72 Cal. L. Rev. 753 (1984) (urging a similar but distinctive analogical approach); Note, *Toward a Constitutional Definition of Religion*, 91 Harv. L.

might work for both clauses, but if one departs from a conventional definition, some type of dual or variable approach might indeed be appropriate. For example, relying on changing values and understandings of the sort described in *Seeger*, one can argue that the contemporary Free Exercise Clause should protect claims of conscience that are not conventionally religious as well as those that are. But the changes discussed in *Seeger* are not necessarily relevant to the Establishment Clause, which serves different functions. Thus, even if religion is defined broadly for the purpose of evaluating legal burdens under the Free Exercise Clause, perhaps the Establishment Clause should limit the award of legal benefits only when the benefitted organizations or practices are conventionally religious. A dual approach along these lines, however, is not without problems. Notably, it might create an unbalanced doctrine that actually favors unconventional over conventional religion by granting it Free Exercise protection, but not the offsetting disadvantages that spring from Establishment Clause limitations.

For now, all we can say is that the constitutional definition of religion remains unsettled. It certainly includes conventional religion, as the Founders had assumed it would. It might—or might not—also include a broader set of moral beliefs and practices that are not conventionally religious, but, if so, this

Rev. 1056 (1978) (urging a *Seeger*-like approach for purposes of the Free Exercise Clause, but a more narrow definition under the Establishment Clause).

broader definition might be limited to the Free Exercise Clause. In the chapters that follow, we will focus on cases involving conventional, theistic religion, because that is the nature of the cases the Supreme Court has decided. Even so, it is important to remember that the definitional issue lingers, and its lurking presence may influence the content and direction of the Court's doctrine.

The Content and Sincerity of Religious Beliefs: Prohibited and Permissible Judicial Inquiries

The Supreme Court's reluctance to define religion is paired with, and perhaps related to, its longstanding rejection of any judicial power to examine the content of religious beliefs or doctrines in order to determine their truth or reasonableness. The leading case, from 1944, is *United States v. Ballard.*[20] In *Ballard*, members of the "I Am" movement had been charged with mail fraud, based in part on their claims that they were divine messengers of a "Saint Germain" and that they possessed supernatural healing powers. The Court reasoned that the Religion Clauses forbid the government, including the judiciary, from adopting or rejecting any particular religious creed. (Any such governmental declaration could be viewed as a form of forbidden sectarian discrimination.) Thus, the Court ruled that in deciding the issue of fraud, the jury could not be in-

20. 322 U.S. 78 (1944).

structed to decide the truth or falsity of the defendants' religious assertions, however "incredible" or "preposterous" they might seem. Citing more common religious beliefs, including beliefs about Biblical miracles, the divinity of Christ, and the power of prayer, the Court noted that "[m]en may believe what they cannot prove" and "may not be put to the proof of their religious doctrines or beliefs."[21]

More recently, in the 1981 Free Exercise case of *Thomas v. Review Board*,[22] the Supreme Court stated that "religious beliefs need not be acceptable, logical, consistent, or comprehensible to others in order to merit First Amendment protection."[23] In *Thomas*, the Court ruled that a Jehovah's Witness was free to decide for himself, without judicial second-guessing, whether his religion precluded employment in the direct production of weapons—even if others, including other Jehovah's Witnesses, might think his religious understanding incorrect or unreasonable. More recently still, the Court has gone even further, suggesting that the judiciary should avoid inquiries not only into the truth or reasonableness of religious beliefs, but also into their importance or "centrality" for the religious believer or religious group.[24] Relatedly, in the context of property disputes within or between religious groups or denominations, the Court has said

21. *Id.* at 86–87.

22. 450 U.S. 707 (1981).

23. *Id.* at 714.

24. *See* Hernandez v. Commissioner, 490 U.S. 680, 699 (1989); Employment Div. v. Smith, 494 U.S. 872, 886–87 (1990).

that courts can utilize "neutral principles of law, developed for use in all property disputes," but cannot interpret "particular church doctrines and the importance of those doctrines to the religion."[25]

By contrast, the Supreme Court has indicated that courts are free to evaluate the *sincerity* of religious claims. In *Ballard*, for instance, the Court ruled that in determining the question of fraud, the jury could not address the truth of the defendants' religious claims, but could consider whether the defendants *sincerely believed* their own statements to be true. Likewise, in *Thomas*, the Court noted that the Free Exercise Clause was properly limited to "honest" religious convictions. Without a requirement of judicially tested sincerity, dishonest religious claims, including fraudulent claims for Free Exercise protection, potentially could be asserted at will. Yet the inquiry into sincerity is problematic, because it is difficult to cabin: how is a court or jury to evaluate sincerity without considering the underlying content of the religious claim and whether the claim seems true, or at least reasonable enough to be sincerely believed? Does not a test of sincerity inevitably favor the familiar beliefs of traditional and mainstream religions over the unorthodox views of new and unusual ones? This risk of improper favoritism is indeed substantial, but courts generally have been sensitive to the problem and have been reluctant to dispute the

25. Presbyterian Church in the United States v. Mary Elizabeth Blue Hull Memorial Presbyterian Church, 393 U.S. 440, 449–50 (1969); *see also* Jones v. Wolf, 443 U.S. 595 (1979).

sincerity of religious claims. More generally, the problem is mitigated by the contemporary Supreme Court's emphasis on the value of formal equality implemented through a doctrinal test of nondiscrimination. Whatever its other weaknesses, that approach limits the significance of the sincerity issue by minimizing special treatment for religion, whether sincere or otherwise.

Doctrinal Fundamentals and Doctrinal Elaborations

This chapter has highlighted general concepts and principles under the Religion Clauses. Even at this general level, we have seen a doctrine that is unsettled and problematic. But despite the uncertainties and problems, our discussion of doctrinal fundamentals provides a framework for the more specific doctrinal inquiries that follow. In the next two chapters, we will build upon this framework as we examine, in turn, the Supreme Court's Free Exercise and Establishment Clause decisionmaking.

CHAPTER 5

INTERPRETING THE FREE EXERCISE CLAUSE

The Free Exercise Clause, originally directed to Congress and later extended to the states, precludes the government from "prohibiting the free exercise" of religion. We have already discussed, in Chapter 4, the conundrum of defining religion. But even assuming a conventional or other agreed definition of religion, what constitutes "the free exercise" of religion, and what constitutes a law that unconstitutionally "prohibits" it?

As discussed in Chapter 3, the Religion Clauses can be understood to protect a variety of constitutional values. First and foremost is the value of religious voluntarism, the freedom of individuals to make religious choices for themselves, free from governmental compulsion or inappropriate influence. A robust interpretation of the Free Exercise Clause surely would honor and build upon this value. Extended to organizational behavior, a strong interpretation also would protect a related but distinct constitutional value, the autonomy of religious institutions. In addition, a vigorous Free Exercise doctrine would respect the religious identity of individuals and would permit religion to flourish in the private domain, free from the contaminating effects of governmental authority. It also would serve the value of religious equality, but not necessarily in the sense of formal equality and not to the exclusion of other values. As we will see, however, the Supreme Court in recent years has rejected a robust interpretation of the Free Exercise Clause, favoring instead a far more minimal view. In so doing, the Court has emphasized the value of formal equality and has given only limited weight to religious voluntarism and other constitutional values.

In our discussion of the Court's doctrine, we will first examine the protection of religious beliefs and the freedom to express them through religious speech. We will then consider what sorts of conduct, beyond speech, might also warrant protection as the "exercise" of religion, and we will discuss the types of laws or governmental action affecting religion that might constitute "prohibiting the free exercise thereof." We will address governmental burdens on religious conduct, including burdens that discriminate against religion and those that do not. Discriminatory burdens generally are unconstitutional. By contrast, under current doctrine, nondiscriminatory burdens generally are not impermissible and, indeed, they normally do not even raise a Free Exercise issue. This restrictive interpretation of the Free Exercise Clause has triggered legislative responses, which will be described at the end of the chapter.

Freedom of Belief (and Freedom of Speech)

The Supreme Court has held that freedom of religious *belief* is absolutely protected by the Free Exercise Clause and that this absolute protection extends to disbelief as well, meaning that the Clause to this extent shelters religion and irreligion alike. Here, the value of religious voluntarism is paramount and controlling, and it is implemented through a doctrinal principle that precludes the government from mandating, prohibiting, or regulating religious or irreligious beliefs as such. In its 1961 decision in *Torcaso v. Watkins*,[1] the Supreme Court relied on this principle to invalidate a religious oath requirement for state office holders, thereby reading the Free Exercise Clause to mirror Article VI of the original Constitution, which explicitly bans such religious tests, but only for *federal* offices. "[N]either a State nor the Federal Government," wrote the Court, "can constitutionally force a person 'to profess a belief or disbelief in any religion.' "[2]

As *Torcaso* suggests, the Free Exercise Clause protects not only the right to hold religious or irreligious beliefs, but also the right to declare them or to refuse to do so. These rights are basic and important. Needless to say, religious liberty would be impoverished if we did not protect religious

1. 367 U.S. 488 (1961).

2. *Id.* at 495 (quoting Everson v. Board of Educ., 330 U.S. 1, 15 (1947)).

belief, religious disbelief, and the profession or denial of either. Yet freedom of belief, however fundamental, is rarely an issue. As a practical matter, it is virtually impossible—in the absence of incredibly coercive and intrusive means—to control the inner thoughts that people hold, and, thankfully, our contemporary government is not inclined to make the effort. To be sure, the open expression of religious or irreligious beliefs is more readily subject to regulation. But because the First Amendment independently protects freedom of speech, it is not clear that the Free Exercise Clause is needed to prevent such regulation. For that matter, the Clause is not necessarily essential, even in theory, for the protection of internal belief. Without regard to the Free Exercise Clause, freedom of speech protects the right to both hold and express beliefs, whether religious or otherwise. Free speech doctrine in fact provides important protection for religious speech, as the following discussion will explain. Because free speech does most of the work, however, the Free Exercise Clause has limited significance in this context.

Although our focus in this book is on the Religion Clauses, it is important to highlight the relevance of free speech doctrine, because freedom of religious speech is a fundamental component of religious liberty in the United States. And although this constitutional protection is primarily a matter of free speech, the Free Exercise Clause may play an indirect role. As *Torcaso* implies, religious speech is not just speech, but also the exercise of religion. Its dual constitutional status may support the favored status of religious speech under free speech doctrine, as well as the Court's strong protection of such speech from discriminatory treatment.

In any event, private religious speech, including religious worship, is regarded as fully protected, high-value speech under the First Amendment, subject only to the same free speech tests and analyses that apply to core political speech.[3] Free speech doctrine provides only limited protection against the content-neutral regulation of speech, including religious speech,[4] but it strongly disfavors content-based regulation and especially viewpoint-based discrimination. Notably, governmental action that formally or deliberately discriminates against religious speech is almost always treated as not only content-based, but also viewpoint-based. As a matter of free speech doctrine, this finding triggers extremely strict scrutiny of not only regulatory penalties, but also governmental attempts to selectively deny religious speakers access to public property that serves as a forum for private speech—including even property that is not, by tradition or designation, a full-fledged "public forum" under free speech principles.

3. *See, e.g.,* Widmar v. Vincent, 454 U.S. 263, 269 (1981); Capitol Square Review & Advisory Bd. v. Pinette, 515 U.S. 753, 760 (1995).

4. Even content-neutral regulation is impermissible in certain contexts, and this protection extends to religious speech. *See, e.g.,* Watchtower Bible & Tract Soc'y of N.Y., Inc. v. Village of Stratton, 536 U.S. 150 (2002) (invalidating a content-neutral permit requirement for door-to-door canvassing, which reached Jehovah's Witnesses among others).

The Supreme Court has developed and applied this analysis in a series of "equal access" cases involving claims by religious speakers that they have been improperly denied access to public property. In these cases, the religious claimants have challenged policies permitting the after-hours use of public buildings by secular groups or for secular purposes, but expressly precluding such use by religious groups or for religious purposes. The claimants rely on free speech, typically asserting viewpoint discrimination. The government denies it, but goes on to argue that even if there were a presumptive violation of free speech, the Establishment Clause would preclude the requested access to the public property. Honoring the Establishment Clause by excluding the religious speakers, the government contends, serves a compelling interest that satisfies free speech doctrine even if strict scrutiny is required.

In deciding these cases, the Supreme Court generally has accepted the challengers' free speech argument and rejected the government's Establishment Clause defense, essentially by finding that the government's fear of breaching the Establishment Clause is misplaced, because equal access for religious and secular speech would not be a violation.[5] The Court recently has extended this reasoning to after-school religious meetings at public schools, even for elementary students.[6] Moving beyond phys-

5. *See, e.g., Widmar*, 454 U.S. 263; Lamb's Chapel v. Center Moriches Union Free School Dist., 508 U.S. 384 (1993).

6. Good News Club v. Milford Central School, 533 U.S. 98 (2001).

ical facilities, the Court also has applied its equal access reasoning to public property in the form of financial support, holding in *Rosenberger v. Rector and Visitors of the University of Virginia*[7] that the University of Virginia could not deny "student activities" funding for a student group's Christian publication. *Rosenberger* does not authorize free speech challenges to discriminatory funding programs in general, but it does support such challenges when the government funds a broad and diverse range of private speech, thereby creating a "metaphysical" free speech forum.[8]

The Establishment Clause reasoning in the Court's equal access cases is important and controversial, and it is a topic to which we will return in the next chapter. The key point here is that one type of religious exercise—private religious speech—has been accorded substantial constitutional protection, albeit largely as a matter of free speech and largely in the context of governmental action that formally or deliberately discriminates against religion.[9]

7. 515 U.S. 819 (1995).

8. The Court emphasized this distinction in *Locke v. Davey*, 540 U.S. 712 (2004), ruling that *Rosenberger* did not extend to a state-sponsored college scholarship program that excluded students who majored in devotional theology. According to the Court, the scholarship program was "not a forum for speech" because it was designed to assist students with the cost of their education, "not to ' "encourage a diversity of views from private speakers." ' " *Id.* at 720 n.3 (citations omitted). We will consider *Locke* more fully in later sections of this chapter.

9. The government's own speech, that is, governmental speech—although subject to the Establishment Clause—does not

What, then, of the Free Exercise Clause? If the Clause offers nothing more than freedom of belief and profession, it does little if anything that freedom of speech does not. In early cases, the Supreme Court suggested that the Free Exercise Clause in fact does nothing more and that, in particular, it provides no protection for religious conduct (other than speech). Thus, in its 1879 decision in *Reynolds v. United States*,[10] the Court held that the Free Exercise Clause did not protect the Mormon practice of polygamy. "Laws are made for the government of actions," the Court wrote, "and while they cannot interfere with mere religious belief and opinions, they may with practices," lest "every citizen ... become a law unto himself."[11] According to

trigger a free speech right to nondiscriminatory treatment or equal access. Permanent monuments on public property, for instance, normally are governmental speech even if the monuments were originally donated by private groups. As to such monuments, there can be Establishment Clause challenges (as we will see in the next chapter), but there is no forum for private speech and therefore no right of equal access. In a questionable decision that is to be reviewed by the Supreme Court, however, the United States Court of Appeals for the Tenth Circuit recently ruled otherwise, permitting an equal access challenge by a minority religious group seeking to place its own monument in a city park containing a privately donated Ten Commandments monument. *See* Summum v. Pleasant Grove City, 483 F.3d 1044 (10th Cir. 2007), *cert. granted*, ___ U.S. ___, 128 S.Ct. 1737 (2008). It appears that Judge McConnell had the better view in his opinion urging the Tenth Circuit to rehear the case en banc. *See* Summum v. Pleasant Grove City, 499 F.3d 1170, 1174–78 (10th Cir. 2007) (McConnell, J., dissenting from denial of rehearing en banc).

10. 98 U.S. 145 (1879).

11. *Id.* at 166–67.

Reynolds, citizens have the right to *believe* in a religious practice such as polygamy, and they have the freedom to express their opinion through speech. Yet they are not free to act on their belief by actually engaging in the religious conduct. Needless to say, this is an extremely narrow, if not barren, interpretation of the Free Exercise Clause. This narrow view was later abandoned by the Supreme Court and, despite more recent doctrinal retrenchment, the Clause today offers some additional protection.

Religious Conduct and Substantial Burdens

A more vibrant understanding of the Free Exercise Clause would protect religious conduct, that is, the freedom to act in accordance with one's religious beliefs. Unlike the protection of belief, this protection certainly could not be absolute; imagine, for example, the act of religiously motivated human sacrifice. But as a matter of presumptive constitutional protection, the Free Exercise Clause would move beyond mere belief, granting individuals a much more meaningful liberty—the freedom not only to decide what they *should* do religiously, but also to do it. The constitutional value of religious voluntarism would seem to demand no less. This protection likewise would honor and respect the religious identity of individuals, a value that is closely related to voluntarism but that identifies an aspect of human dignity that does not necessarily require the exercise of autonomous choice. Indeed, many individuals do not believe that they independently "choose" their own religion; rather, it is chosen for them by God, or perhaps by another religious force. Respecting their religious identity, and according them religious equality, means that even if these citizens attribute their religious decisions and actions to a source beyond themselves, they should receive no less Free Exercise protection than citizens with a more autonomous belief structure. Protecting religious conduct also would further other constitutional values, including religious flourishing in the private domain and the autonomy of religious institutions in demanding or encouraging particular forms of religious behavior.

As we will discuss shortly, the contemporary Supreme Court does not give the Free Exercise Clause a forceful interpretation. Despite its otherwise restrictive view, however, the Court does recognize that the exercise of religion includes religious conduct: "The free exercise of religion means, first and foremost, the right to believe and profess whatever religious doctrine one desires.... But the 'exercise of religion' often involves not only belief and profession but the performance of (or abstention from) physical acts: assembling with others for a worship service, participating in sacramental use of bread and wine, proselytizing, abstaining from certain foods or certain modes of transportation."[12] As a matter of current doctrine, the exercise of religion

12.   Employment Div. v. Smith, 494 U.S. 872, 877 (1990).

thus includes religious conduct, including but not limited to religious speech.

This conclusion advances the inquiry, but certainly does not end it. One must determine, more precisely, what type of religious conduct (or abstention)[13] qualifies as the exercise of religion. And even if religious conduct is the exercise of religion, it might still fall outside the scope of the Free Exercise Clause. As a textual matter, for example, one might say that not all religious "exercise" is within the constitutionally protected "*free* exercise" or (as the current Court prefers) that not all governmental intrusions qualify as "prohibitions." But this may be little more than semantics. However closely or cleverly one reads the text, it does not answer the key substantive questions. In particular, one must determine what a challenger must show in order to trigger presumptive constitutional protection under the Free Exercise Clause, and one then must determine the precise nature of that presumptive protection.

In the remainder of this section, we will focus on the Supreme Court's contemporary doctrine concerning what amounts to the first stage of the "triggering" inquiry. More specifically, we will examine each of two initial requirements for triggering presumptive protection under the Free Exercise Clause: first, the claimant must be engaging in religious conduct that qualifies as the exercise of

13. For simplicity, this discussion will focus on affirmative religious conduct. The concepts and principles are no different for religious abstention.

religion within the scope of the Clause; and second, the governmental action must constitute a burden on this religious exercise that is substantial enough to be constitutionally cognizable. (Even if these initial requirements are met, there still is no presumptive protection, in general, unless the burden on religious exercise is discriminatory, an issue that will be discussed in following sections.)

For conduct to qualify as the exercise of religion under the Free Exercise Clause, the conduct must, at a minimum, be conduct that is sincerely motivated by religious beliefs. As discussed in Chapter 4, religious beliefs for this purpose at least include beliefs derived from conventional, theistic religion, but may also include a broader set of moral convictions. In any event, the claimant must be sincere in two respects: he or she must sincerely accept the religious belief as true or genuine and, in addition, it must be that belief—and not secular self-interest, for example—that actually motivates the conduct in question.

The requirements of religious motivation and sincerity are important and necessary, but they may not be sufficient. Even assuming a conventional definition of religion, conduct is often motivated by religious beliefs, at least partially, and most religious claimants are undeniably sincere. Under these criteria, qualifying conduct might include not only such inherently religious acts as prayer, worship, and ritual, but also a much broader variety of conduct inspired by religious understandings of morality or ethics. Without additional limitations, the exercise of religion might be so expansively defined that meaningful constitutional protection would be unrealistic. As a result, it might be appropriate to impose additional requirements, requirements limiting the scope of religious exercise to conduct that is especially important to religious voluntarism, religious identity, and other constitutional values.

The Supreme Court has at times suggested two such additional requirements. First, it sometimes has suggested that the religious conduct protected by the Free Exercise Clause is that which is "central" to a religion, or at least that which the claimant sincerely believes to be central. Second, it sometimes has spoken of conduct that is not merely religiously motivated, but that is *compelled* or *mandated* by the claimant's sincere understanding of religious duty or obligation. More recently, however, the Court has emphasized that any judicial inquiry into centrality is improper, stating that such an inquiry is no more permissible than a judicial inquiry into religious truth. Although the Court could still require a *sincere claim* of religious centrality, it has implied that it will not do so.[14] And it has continued to speak not only of conduct that is religiously compelled, but also of conduct that is religiously motivated, giving no clear indication of

14. *See Smith*, 494 U.S. at 886–88. *But cf.* Hernandez v. Commissioner, 490 U.S. 680, 699 (1989) (declaring that the judiciary cannot determine centrality, but implying that a sincere claim of centrality may be required); Church of the Lukumi Babalu Aye, Inc. v. City of Hialeah, 508 U.S. 520, 534 (1993) (affording Free Exercise protection to "the central element" of Santeria worship).

how strong or substantial the religious motivation must be.[15]

As later sections of the chapter will show, the contemporary Supreme Court has severely limited Free Exercise protection, but not through the device of defining religious exercise restrictively. Thus, like "religion" for Free Exercise purposes, the "exercise" of religion has neither been clearly defined nor narrowly limited by the Supreme Court. Perhaps the best reading of the Court's uncertain doctrine is that the exercise of religion requires neither centrality nor religious compulsion, but that it does demand, implicitly, that a claimant be sincerely relying on a religious belief as the *primary* or *dominant* motivation for the conduct in question. If so, this would still be a relatively lenient requirement, and virtually any serious claimant could meet it.

Assuming that a claimant's conduct qualifies as the exercise of religion, what amounts to a constitutionally cognizable burden on that exercise? The Supreme Court has stated that the burden must be a "substantial burden,"[16] but, here again, the Court has not explained exactly what this means. What is clear is that two different sorts of burdens can be

15. *See, e.g., Smith*, 494 U.S. at 876, 877, 878, 888 (referring variously to "conduct required by ... religion," "acts ... engaged in for religious reasons," conduct grounded in "religious motivation," acts "require[d]" by religious belief, and "actions thought to be religiously commanded"); *Lukumi*, 508 U.S. at 524, 532, 546 (referring to ceremonies "command[ed]" by religion, but also to "conduct motivated by religious beliefs" and "conduct with a religious motivation").

16. *See, e.g., Hernandez*, 490 U.S. at 699.

substantial enough to be constitutionally cognizable: burdens that are "direct" and those that are "indirect."[17]

A direct burden arises when the exercise of religion unavoidably triggers a criminal sanction or other legal penalty. Typically, the effect of the law is to forbid the religious conduct, making it literally impossible for the religious claimant to honor both the law and his or her religious understandings. *Wisconsin v. Yoder*[18] provides an example. Wisconsin's compulsory education law required parents to send their children to school until the age of 16. Old Order Amish could not follow the law, however, without abandoning a religious obligation: protecting their children from the worldly influences of high school. As the Court noted, the law's impact on the Amish parents' religious exercise was "not only severe, but inescapable," because it "affirmatively compell[ed] them, under threat of criminal sanction, to perform acts undeniably at odds with fundamental tenets of their religious beliefs."[19] The Court protected the Amish from this direct burden by recognizing a constitutionally required exemption from the law.

An indirect burden arises when the law does not unavoidably regulate or forbid religious exercise but does place a religious believer on the horns of a decisional dilemma, for example, by offering finan-

17. This direct-versus-indirect dichotomy can be understood in various ways. What follows is one interpretation.

18. 406 U.S. 205 (1972).

19. *Id.* at 218.

cial or other benefits under conditions that would require the believer to forego his or her religious conduct. In *Sherbert v. Verner*,[20] for instance, unemployment compensation was available only to those who would accept Saturday employment. The Court granted Free Exercise protection to a Saturday Sabbatarian, ruling that the Saturday-work condition could not be applied to her. The Court noted that although the burden might properly be described as "indirect," the law nonetheless exerted "unmistakable" pressure on the exercise of religion by forcing the claimant "to choose between following the precepts of her religion and forfeiting benefits, on the one hand, and abandoning one of the precepts of her religion in order to accept work, on the other hand."[21] More recently, in *Locke v. Davey*,[22] a case to which we will return shortly, the Court addressed a Free Exercise challenge to a state-sponsored college scholarship program. The program denied funding to students who elected to major in devotional theology, thereby creating an indirect burden on their religious decisionmaking. Unlike in *Sherbert*, however, the Court found the burden "relatively minor,"[23] and, for that reason among others, it rejected the Free Exercise challenge.

Direct and indirect burdens each can impair various constitutional values, but the Court's analysis

20. 374 U.S. 398 (1963).

21. *Id.* at 403–04.

22. 540 U.S. 712 (2004).

23. *Id.* at 725.

of whether a burden is substantial enough to be constitutionally cognizable appears to rest primarily on the value of religious voluntarism and, more specifically, on the protection of religious conscience. A direct burden on the exercise of religion obviously intrudes upon religious conscience and voluntarism by impeding the freedom to make and implement religious choices. In certain circumstances, however, an indirect burden might exert as great, or potentially greater, coercive pressure on this religious decisionmaking. A restrictive condition can be attached to substantial financial benefits, whereas the violation of a direct legal ban might lead to a minimal fine. In *Yoder*, for example, the Amish parents confronted a criminal sanction, but had been fined only $5.00. Whatever the precise penalty, however, a direct burden can force nonconforming religious believers to defy the law, thus bearing the opprobrium of unlawful conduct and, in the case of a criminal law, the brand of criminality. In any event, a burden, whether direct or indirect, presumably qualifies as substantial if it dissuades or discourages the exercise of religion by exerting substantial coercive pressure on religious decisionmaking.

Conversely, the Supreme Court has suggested, controversially, that there is no constitutionally cognizable burden when governmental action does not impair religious voluntarism by influencing *religious decisionmaking*, even if the governmental action might significantly impede the exercise of religion in other ways. In *Lyng v. Northwest Indian Cemetery Protective Association*,[24] for example, the Court found that no cognizable burden would result from a proposed National Forest road that, according to the challengers, would have seriously damaged the sanctity of Native American sacred sites. The Court conceded that the proposed road would "have severe adverse effects" on the challengers' ability to practice their religion at the sacred sites, but it emphasized that they would not "be coerced by the Government's action into violating their religious beliefs."[25] In terms of religious voluntarism, the governmental action would not induce the Native American believers to make or forego any religious decision concerning the conduct in which they should engage (even if that conduct might no longer be religiously efficacious or even possible!), and it therefore would not impede their exercise of religious conscience. This type of reasoning, however, ignores other constitutional values, including the protection of religious identity as an aspect of human dignity. Perhaps most important, it fails to accord religious equality to religious understandings that do not emphasize individual responsibility and personal choice.[26]

24.   485 U.S. 439 (1988).

25.   *Id.* at 447, 449. The Court further suggested that the Free Exercise Clause generally does not restrict the government's internal operations and affairs. *See id.* at 448–49; *see also* Bowen v. Roy, 476 U.S. 693, 699–701 (1986).

26.   *See* David C. Williams & Susan H. Williams, *Volitionalism and Religious Liberty*, 76 Cornell L. Rev. 769 (1991).

Nondiscriminatory Burdens on Religious Conduct

Under the constitutional regime exemplified by *Wisconsin v. Yoder* and *Sherbert v. Verner*, a constitutionally substantial burden on the exercise of religion was enough, without more, to trigger presumptive protection under the Free Exercise Clause, giving rise to searching judicial scrutiny even when the burden resulted from a nondiscriminatory, generally applicable law. If the government could not satisfy this scrutiny in defending the law's application to the challenger's religious conduct, an exemption from the law was constitutionally required. This regime prevailed from 1963, when the Supreme Court decided *Sherbert*, until 1990, when the Court decided *Employment Division v. Smith*.[27]

The Court's language in *Sherbert* and *Yoder* suggested full-fledged strict scrutiny, with an exemption required unless the law's application to the religious conduct was necessary to serve a "compelling state interest" or an "interest[] of the highest order."[28] In reality, however, the test was not as strict as it sounded, and the Court sometimes rejected exemption claims in opinions that implied a somewhat more lenient approach.[29] The Court also

27. 494 U.S. 872 (1990).

28. Sherbert v. Verner, 374 U.S. 398, 403 (1963); Wisconsin v. Yoder, 406 U.S. 205, 215 (1972).

29. *See, e.g.,* United States v. Lee, 455 U.S. 252, 257–60 (1982); Bob Jones Univ. v. United States, 461 U.S. 574, 603–04 (1983).

recognized explicit exceptions to strict scrutiny for military and prison regulations, which it evaluated under a reasonableness or rational-basis standard.[30] Outside these exceptional areas, however, the Court continued to endorse a relatively demanding standard of review throughout the 1980s. In thus protecting the exercise of religion even from nondiscriminatory burdens, the Court's doctrine reflected a variety of constitutional values, but most of all the value of religious voluntarism. As suggested in the previous section, that value is seriously impaired whenever there is a substantial burden on the exercise of religion, and it matters not whether the burden results from a discriminatory law.

Employment Division v. Smith marked a dramatic turn in doctrine. In *Smith*, the Court was asked to recognize a Free Exercise exemption for the sacramental use of an otherwise illegal drug, peyote, by members of the Native American Church. Not only did the Court refuse to do so, but, over the strong objection of four justices, it also declined to apply the scrutiny that *Sherbert* and *Yoder* appeared to demand. Although the Court purported to distinguish and preserve its particular holdings in those cases, it essentially renounced their fundamental teaching. Thus, the Court declared that general laws affecting religious conduct do not require any form of heightened scrutiny and therefore do not require religious exemptions.

30. Goldman v. Weinberger, 475 U.S. 503, 507–08 (1986) (military); O'Lone v. Estate of Shabazz, 482 U.S. 342, 348–50 (1987) (prisons).

Giving a narrow reading to the word "prohibiting" in the Free Exercise Clause, the Court rejected the argument "that 'prohibiting the free exercise [of religion]' includes requiring any individual to observe a generally applicable law that requires (or forbids) the performance of an act that his religious belief forbids (or requires)."[31] Harkening back to its 1879 opinion in *Reynolds*, the Court suggested that to grant a Free Exercise exemption from a general law would be to permit the religious believer, "by virtue of his beliefs, 'to become a law unto himself,' " a result that "contradicts both constitutional tradition and common sense."[32] The Court especially objected to the prospect of balancing religious claims against competing state interests in a wide variety of possible contexts, a task for which, according to the Court, judges are not well-suited.

As discussed in the previous section, the initial requirements for triggering presumptive Free Exercise protection are twofold: the challenger's conduct must qualify as the exercise of religion, and the challenged governmental action must constitute a substantial burden on that religious exercise. Under the doctrine of *Smith*, however, these showings are merely preliminary, because a nondiscriminatory burden on the exercise of religion, no matter how substantial, generally does not implicate the Free Exercise Clause. As we will see, there are some

31. *Smith*, 494 U.S. at 878 (bracketed language provided by the Court).

32. *Id.* at 885 (quoting Reynolds v. United States, 98 U.S. 145, 167 (1879)).

possible refinements or exceptions to the basic approach of *Smith*, but it appears that the Free Exercise Clause today is limited primarily if not entirely to discriminatory burdens. And it further appears that such burdens arise only from laws that formally or deliberately discriminate against religion. By immunizing most or all nondiscriminatory burdens from Free Exercise scrutiny, *Smith* severely undermines the constitutional value of religious voluntarism. At the same time, it dramatically elevates the value of religious equality, understood in a strictly formal sense.

Discriminatory Burdens on Religious Conduct

Under the doctrine of *Smith*, a burden on the exercise of religion triggers presumptive constitutional protection if the burden is not only substantial, but also discriminatory. According to the Supreme Court, a burden is discriminatory if it results from a law that is tainted by "the unconstitutional object of targeting religious beliefs and practices."[33] This language—and most of the Court's reasoning in *Smith* and later cases—suggests that the touchstone is formal or deliberate discrimination, directed either against a particular religion or against religion in general. Under this approach, the Free Exercise Clause is reduced to a provision analogous to the Fourteenth Amendment's Equal Protection Clause, which protects against purposeful discrimi-

33. City of Boerne v. Flores, 521 U.S. 507, 529 (1997).

nation based on impermissible criteria. At least in the contemporary period, however, it is difficult to find laws that purposefully target the exercise of religion for special burdens, leading critics to charge that under the doctrine of *Smith*, the Free Exercise Clause has little if any practical significance.

In fact, *Smith* severely reduced, but did not eliminate, the practical significance of the Clause. As rare as discriminatory burdens may be, they are not nonexistent, as became clear in *Church of the Lukumi Babalu Aye, Inc. v. City of Hialeah*,[34] a case decided only three years after *Smith*. *Lukumi* invalidated a series of ordinances that had been adopted by the City of Hialeah, Florida, in direct response to the proposed establishment of a Santeria church in Hialeah. Santeria, a religion originating in Cuba and combining traditional African religion with elements of Roman Catholicism, practices animal sacrifice as a principal form of devotion. In a transparent attempt to stop the establishment and spread of Santeria, the Hialeah city council made it a crime to "sacrifice" an animal, defined to mean "unnecessarily kill, torment, torture, or mutilate an animal in a public or private ritual or ceremony not for the primary purpose of food consumption." Taken together, the city's overlapping ordinances effectively outlawed the Santeria practice of animal sacrifice even as the ordinances left other animal killings unaffected—including not only secular killings, but also the Orthodox Jewish practice of Kosher slaugh-

34. 508 U.S. 520 (1993).

ter (in part because Kosher slaughter *is* "for the primary purpose of food consumption").

"At a minimum," the Supreme Court wrote in *Lukumi*, "the protections of the Free Exercise Clause pertain if the law at issue discriminates against some or all religious beliefs or regulates or prohibits conduct because it is undertaken for religious reasons."[35] Unlike, for example, a general ban on animal killing (which, under *Smith*, would raise no Free Exercise issue), the Hialeah ordinances specifically targeted Santeria religious exercise and, as such, imposed a burden that was not only direct and substantial, but also discriminatory. This discriminatory burden triggered presumptive constitutional protection and demanded "the most rigorous of scrutiny."[36] *Lukumi* involved sectarian discrimination—discrimination not against religion in general but against the particular religion of Santeria. The Court's reasoning, however, extended to all discriminatory burdens, whether sectarian or nonsectarian in nature.[37] The Court noted that a "compelling governmental interest" and a "narrowly tailored" law conceivably might justify a discriminatory burden, but it went on to state that these requirements would be satisfied "only in rare cases."[38] In reality, it is hard to imagine why the

35. *Id.* at 532.

36. *Id.* at 546.

37. *Cf.* McDaniel v. Paty, 435 U.S. 618 (1978) (invalidating a state law that prohibited the clergy of any denomination from holding designated public offices).

38. *See Lukumi*, 508 U.S. at 531–32, 546–47.

government would ever find it necessary to target religious exercise for discriminatory treatment, at least in the imposition of a direct burden. Indeed, a law that imposes a direct and discriminatory burden on the exercise of religion typically has no constitutional applications, rendering the law invalid on its face.

What about indirect burdens? As *Sherbert* makes clear, conditions on the award of financial or other benefits can pressure would-be recipients to forego religious choices, placing them on the horns of a decisional dilemma and creating a substantial burden on the exercise of religion. Even after *Smith*, moreover, *Lukumi* would appear to demand vigorous judicial review if such an indirect burden is discriminatory—that is, if the government is formally or deliberately discriminating against religion by refusing benefits precisely because the would-be recipients are religious or because they would be using the benefits to pursue religious activities. To be sure, not all indirect burdens exert substantial coercive pressure on religious decisionmaking. But when the government deliberately discriminates against religion in the selective award of benefits, it impairs not only religious voluntarism but also religious equality. As a result, one could argue that virtually any burden, if discriminatory, should be treated as sufficiently substantial to trigger presumptive protection under the Free Exercise Clause.

An argument along these lines persuaded the United States Court of Appeals for the Ninth Circuit,[39] but, to the surprise of many, a seven-justice Supreme Court majority reversed the Ninth Circuit in *Locke v. Davey*,[40] decided in 2004. In *Locke*, the Court considered a State of Washington program that provided merit- and income-based scholarships, ranging from about $1,000 to about $1,500 per year, to students at public and private colleges, but that denied the scholarships to otherwise eligible students at religious colleges if they were majoring in devotional theology, typically to prepare for careers in the ministry. For reasons we will address in the next chapter, this discriminatory, religion-based denial of funding was not required by the Establishment Clause, which would have permitted Washington to extend the scholarships to the ministry students who were excluded. But the state relied on a provision in Washington's state constitution, which mandated a stronger separation of church and state, and Supreme Court permitted the state's anti-establishment policy to prevail.

According to the Court, " 'there is room for play in the joints' " between the Establishment and Free Exercise Clauses,[41] meaning that states sometimes are free, if they choose, to promote anti-establishment policies that go beyond what the Establishment Clause demands. Here, Washington's discriminatory denial of scholarship funding created an obvious disincentive—a "financial penalty," in the

39. *See* Davey v. Locke, 299 F.3d 748 (9th Cir. 2002), *rev'd*, 540 U.S. 712 (2004).

40. 540 U.S. 712 (2004).

41. *Id.* at 718 (quoting Walz v. Tax Comm'n, 397 U.S. 664, 669 (1970)).

words of Justice Scalia's dissent[42]—for any student otherwise inclined to pursue a religious calling. Even so, in a finding seemingly at odds with *Sherbert*, the Court concluded that the burden on religious exercise was "relatively minor."[43] As a result, the Court rejected the strict scrutiny of *Lukumi* in favor of a far more lenient balancing approach. And under that approach, the state's denial of funding was justified by historical anti-establishment concerns about taxpayer-supported clergy, concerns that were reflected in a number of state constitutions.

The scope of *Locke* remains to be seen. It might be limited to the selective denial of funding for the devotional religious work and training of clergy and other religious professionals. Under this interpretation, the Free Exercise Clause might still preclude, in other settings, the exclusion of religious options from otherwise general programs of funding, such as voucher-based programs for education or social services. But the Court's emphasis on "play in the joints" might suggest a broader interpretation of *Locke*, one that would give the states considerable leeway.[44]

42. *Id.* at 731 (Scalia, J., dissenting).

43. *Id.* at 725 (majority opinion). The Court claimed that unlike in *Sherbert*, individuals were not required "to choose between their religious beliefs and receiving a government benefit" because students majoring in devotional theology still could receive a scholarship, albeit only if they were simultaneously pursuing a secular degree at a separate educational institution. *Id.* at 720–21 & n.4.

44. For lower court decisions interpreting *Locke* broadly and extending its reasoning to uphold state-law exclusions of reli-

Whatever its scope, *Locke* permits governmental action that dissuades and discriminates against religious choices. Perhaps anti-establishment considerations are sufficient to justify this result, but, as discussed in the next chapter, the Supreme Court itself has reasoned otherwise in its interpretations of the Establishment Clause. There, the Court has determined that constitutional values—especially religious voluntarism and religious equality, both formal and substantive—support the nondiscriminatory extension of funding to religious recipients in settings such as this. Thus, it seems that *Locke* is simply giving deference to state-law policymaking in this context, regardless of whether that policymaking fully honors the values of the Religion Clauses.

To summarize, substantial and discriminatory burdens on the exercise of religion trigger an extremely strong presumption of invalidity and extremely strong strict scrutiny. This doctrine applies to direct burdens, as in *Lukumi*. The values of

gious schools from voucher programs for elementary and secondary education, see Eulitt v. Maine, 386 F.3d 344 (1st Cir. 2004); Bush v. Holmes, 886 So.2d 340 (Fla. Dist. Ct. App. 2004) (en banc), *aff'd on other grounds*, 919 So.2d 392 (Fla. 2006). For a critique of *Locke* and an argument that the decision should be interpreted narrowly, see Thomas C. Berg & Douglas Laycock, *The Mistakes in* Locke v. Davey *and the Future of State Payments for Services Provided by Religious Institutions*, 40 Tulsa L. Rev. 227 (2004). *Cf.* Colorado Christian Univ. v. Weaver, 534 F.3d 1245 (10th Cir. 2008) (invalidating a state-sponsored college scholarship program that, unlike in *Locke*, excluded all students attending "pervasively sectarian" religious colleges, with the court concluding that the "pervasively sectarian" criterion discriminated among religions and required an unconstitutionally intrusive religious inquiry).

religious voluntarism and religious equality would support an extension of this doctrine to indirect burdens as well, but *Locke* suggests that the Supreme Court may be disinclined to find that indirect burdens, even if discriminatory, are sufficiently substantial to trigger presumptive Free Exercise protection.

Free Exercise Protection Even in the Absence of Formal or Deliberate Discrimination?

In the context of indirect burdens, contemporary Free Exercise protection is confined by *Locke*. More generally, even in the context of direct and substantial burdens, the controlling doctrine is that of *Smith* and *Lukumi*. This doctrine is designed primarily to redress discriminatory burdens on religious exercise, that is, burdens that are formally or purposefully directed to religious exercise as such. This restrictive approach, which emphasizes nondiscrimination and formal religious equality, clearly is the heart of the Supreme Court's doctrine. Even so, the Court has not entirely foreclosed the possibility of additional Free Exercise protection, which might serve other constitutional values. In particular, the Court has suggested that even in the absence of formal or deliberate discrimination, substantial burdens on the exercise of religion might trigger presumptive constitutional protection in each of three contexts: laws that are not "generally applicable"; "hybrid" cases combining Free Exercise and other constitutional arguments; and cases involving the institutional autonomy of religious organizations.

Smith, Lukumi, and "General Applicability"

In *Smith*, the Court referred to the nondiscriminatory burdens that are immune from Free Exercise challenge as those that result from "neutral law[s] of general applicability."[45] At first glance, it would seem that this phrase, taken as a whole, simply describes laws that do not target religious exercise and that therefore do not reflect formal or deliberate discrimination. According to a more complex interpretation, however, the word "neutral" captures the presumptive prohibition on purposeful discrimination, and "general applicability" means something else. According to this second interpretation, a law that imposes a substantial burden on the exercise of religion can escape Free Exercise scrutiny only if it is not only "neutral"—that is, free from formal or deliberate discrimination—but also "generally applicable"—understood as a separate requirement.

Most of the Court's opinion in *Smith* supports the first interpretation of this phrase. Yet one aspect of the Court's reasoning implied that "general applicability" might indeed be a separate requirement. Thus, in its creative attempt to distinguish *Sherbert* and similar cases concerning unemployment compensation,[46] the Court noted that they involved "a

45. Employment Div. v. Smith, 494 U.S. 872, 879 (1990) (quoting United States v. Lee, 455 U.S. 252, 263 n.3 (1982) (Stevens, J., concurring in the judgment)).

46. *See* Thomas v. Review Bd., 450 U.S. 707 (1981); Hobbie v. Unemployment Appeals Comm'n, 480 U.S. 136 (1987); Frazee v. Illinois Dep't of Employment Sec., 489 U.S. 829 (1989).

context that lent itself to individualized governmental assessment of the reasons for the relevant conduct." The unemployment cases, the Court stated, "stand for the proposition that where the State has in place a system of individual exemptions, it may not refuse to extend that system to cases of 'religious hardship' without compelling reason."[47] The Court thus suggested that laws requiring at least some sorts of "individualized assessment" do not qualify as generally applicable laws and therefore are not immune from Free Exercise challenge. The Court's opinion in *Lukumi* went further, explicitly discussing "general applicability" as a separate requirement and concluding that the Hialeah ordinances did not qualify. The Court noted that the city had legitimate interests in public health and animal protection, but that the ordinances pursued those interests so selectively and "underinclusively" that they reached little if any conduct other than Santeria animal sacrifice.

Relying especially on *Lukumi* and reading "general applicability" as a separate and robust requirement, advocates have argued—and some lower courts have agreed—that the Supreme Court's Free Exercise doctrine can be read to protect religious exercise from various laws that do not purposefully discriminate against it. In particular, they contend that even if a law regulates secular and religious conduct alike, it is presumptively invalid if it imposes a substantial burden on religious exercise and if

47. *Smith*, 494 U.S. at 884.

the law, on its face or as applied, includes secular exceptions that undermine the government's interest in uniformity. Strict scrutiny would follow, and it typically could not be satisfied. Under this interpretation, "[i]f there are exceptions for secular interests, the religious claimant has to be treated as favorably as those who benefit from the secular exceptions."[48] For example, if a police department recognizes medical excuses for the wearing of beards in violation of its facial-hair policy, it must also excuse the wearing of beards as a matter of religious obligation. Likewise, if a state university exempts students from mandatory student housing for various secular reasons, it must exempt a religious objector seeking to live in a religious group home.[49] This interpretation would extend the Free Exercise Clause beyond purposeful discrimination to redress laws that do not target religion, but that reflect selective indifference or selective inattention to religious interests. It would thus move beyond formal equality and at least in the direction of substantive equality. By opening a broader range of laws to Free Exercise challenges, this interpretation also would promote, to that extent, religious voluntarism and other constitutional values.

48. Douglas Laycock, *The Supreme Court and Religious Liberty*, 40 Cath. Law. 25, 35 (2000); *see also* Richard F. Duncan, *Free Exercise is Dead, Long Live Free Exercise:* Smith, Lukumi, *and the General Applicability Requirement*, 3 U. Pa. J. Const. L. 850 (2001).

49. *See* Laycock, *supra* note 48, at 32–34 (discussing Fraternal Order of Police v. City of Newark, 170 F.3d 359 (3d Cir. 1999), and Rader v. Johnston, 924 F.Supp. 1540 (D. Neb. 1996)).

This robust interpretation of "general applicability" is plausible and potentially attractive, but the advocates and lower courts probably are reading too much into the Supreme Court's doctrine. In *Smith*, the Court's discussion of "individualized assessment" was designed to preserve, and to narrowly confine, the Court's prior holdings in the unemployment compensation cases. And in *Lukumi*, the Court did no more than invalidate laws whose disparate impact on religion was so overwhelming that it compelled an inference of purposeful discrimination, that is, the deliberate targeting of a particular religious practice.[50] The Court specifically found that "[t]he record in this case compels the conclusion that suppression of the central element of the Santeria worship service was the object of the ordinances."[51] Thus, as the Court later explained, the fundamental teaching of *Smith* and *Lukumi* is that governmental action violates the Free Exercise Clause when it has "the unconstitutional object of targeting religious beliefs and practices."[52] Even so,

50. For analogous cases in the context of racial discrimination, see Yick Wo v. Hopkins, 118 U.S. 356 (1886); Gomillion v. Lightfoot, 364 U.S. 339 (1960). Because the purposeful discrimination was so obvious in *Lukumi*, the Court did not need to inquire directly into the underlying or subjective "motivation" for the city council's actions. *Compare* Church of the Lukumi Babalu Aye, Inc. v. City of Hialeah, 508 U.S. 520, 540–42 (1993) (opinion of Kennedy, J.) (conducting such an inquiry nonetheless, and concluding that it further demonstrated the existence of purposeful discrimination), *with id.* at 558–59 (Scalia, J., concurring in part and concurring in the judgment) (objecting to this portion of Justice Kennedy's opinion).

51. *Lukumi*, 508 U.S. at 534.

52. City of Boerne v. Flores, 521 U.S. 507, 529 (1997).

the Court's unemployment compensation cases themselves remain valid, and there is room to argue for a broader and more vigorous understanding of general applicability.

"Hybrid" Claims

In *Smith*, the Court suggested that "hybrid" claims—claims that implicate not only the exercise of religion, but also some other constitutional interest—might be viable even against laws that are concededly nondiscriminatory and generally applicable. The Court utilized this theory to distinguish *Wisconsin v. Yoder*, which it described as a "hybrid" case involving not only the Free Exercise Clause, but also the constitutional right of parents to control the education of their children.[53] Like its revisionist interpretation of the unemployment compensation cases, the Court's hybrid-claim theory and its explanation of *Yoder* are tenuous and decidedly post hoc, making one question whether the theory has broader doctrinal significance.[54] If it does, however, it might mean that a substantial burden on the exercise of religion, even if nondiscriminatory, can trigger heightened scrutiny if the law also burdens or impairs another constitutional interest, such as freedom of speech or freedom of association.

53. *See* Employment Div. v. Smith, 494 U.S. 872, 881–82 (1990). The Court cited the substantive due process case of *Pierce v. Society of Sisters*, 268 U.S. 510 (1925), and it noted that *Yoder* had cited *Pierce* as well. *Smith*, 494 U.S. at 881 & n.1.

54. *See* Michael W. McConnell, *Free Exercise Revisionism and the* Smith *Decision*, 57 U. Chi. L. Rev. 1109, 1121–24 (1990).

For the Free Exercise Clause to be doing any work in a hybrid case, of course, the other constitutional claim would have to be inadequate, standing alone, to trigger the same degree of scrutiny. The Supreme Court has done nothing to explain the appropriate constitutional arithmetic, nor has it otherwise elaborated the hybrid-claim theory that it advanced in *Smith*. By all indications, the hybrid-claim theory has limited practical significance. In any event, the Court's doctrine concerning such claims is incomplete and uncertain.

The Institutional Autonomy of Religious Organizations

The institutional autonomy of religious organizations is a constitutional value that is related to, but distinct from, the religious voluntarism of individuals. To a limited extent, the Supreme Court has suggested that this value warrants special constitutional protection. As noted in Chapter 4, the Court has consistently ruled that courts cannot resolve internal disputes involving religious doctrine, a principle that relies in part on Free Exercise considerations, including the value of institutional autonomy. In *Smith*, the Court reaffirmed that government may not "lend its power to one or the other side in controversies over religious authority or dogma."[55] Beyond this, *Smith* does not rule out the possibility of distinctive protection for other aspects of institutional autonomy. For example, the Free Exercise Clause may protect religious organizations in their selection of clergy, notwithstanding employ-

55. *Smith*, 494 U.S. at 877.

ment discrimination laws that would qualify under *Smith* and *Lukumi* as neutral laws of general applicability.[56]

Contemporary Free Exercise doctrine concerning institutional autonomy is uncertain. As with the general applicability requirement and the hybrid-claim theory, however, it seems unlikely that the Court will rely on institutional autonomy to make significant inroads on the basic doctrine of *Smith* and *Lukumi*. As a result, most claims of institutional autonomy are likely to fail unless they involve burdens on the exercise of religion that are not only substantial, but also discriminatory.

Legislative Responses to the Supreme Court's Restrictive Constitutional Doctrine

The Supreme Court's restrictive interpretation of the Free Exercise Clause has generated a remarkable series of legislative responses. In its initial reaction to *Smith*, Congress concluded that the Court's new doctrine gave inadequate protection to the exercise of religion and, indeed, that *Smith*'s interpretation of the Free Exercise Clause was erroneous. Accordingly, Congress attempted to "restore" the

56. *See* Laycock, *supra* note 48, at 36–37. *But cf.* Mark Tushnet, *The Redundant Free Exercise Clause?*, 33 Loy. U. Chi. L.J. 71, 84–86 (2001) (discussing Boy Scouts of America v. Dale, 530 U.S. 640 (2000), and suggesting that without regard to the Free Exercise Clause, a religious organization's selection of its clergy now is constitutionally protected as a matter of expressive association).

prior doctrine of *Sherbert* and *Yoder* by enacting the Religious Freedom Restoration Act of 1993 (RFRA), which declared that "Government shall not substantially burden a person's exercise of religion even if the burden results from a rule of general applicability," unless the government can "demonstrate[] that application of the burden to the person—(1) is in furtherance of a compelling governmental interest; and (2) is the least restrictive means of furthering that compelling governmental interest."[57] RFRA thus demanded strict scrutiny, at least of the *Sherbert/Yoder* variety, for all substantial burdens on religious exercise, including nondiscriminatory burdens—now as a matter of statutory rather than constitutional right.

In 1997, however, in *City of Boerne v. Flores*,[58] the Supreme Court invalidated RFRA, at least in its application to state and local laws and governmental practices, ruling that the Act exceeded Congress's power under Section 5 of the Fourteenth Amendment. As to state and local governments, *Boerne* returned the federal law of religious free exercise to the restrictive constitutional standard of *Smith*. By contrast, although the Court's opinion in *Boerne* was not entirely clear, there is strong reason to believe that RFRA remains valid as applied to federal laws and practices. Indeed, in its recent decision in *Gonzales v. O Centro Espirita Beneficente Uniao do Vegetal*,[59] the Supreme Court not

57. 42 U.S.C. § 2000bb–1 (2006).

58. 521 U.S. 507 (1997).

59. 546 U.S. 418 (2006).

only assumed the constitutionality of RFRA in the federal context, but also offered a vigorous interpretation of the statutory strict scrutiny that RFRA demands.[60] *Boerne* depended in part on the supremacy of the judiciary in constitutional interpretation, but this concern about the separation of powers was linked to a concern about constitutional federalism. Especially in light of *Gonzales*, it seems that *Boerne* was designed to do nothing more than limit Congress's power to impose federal requirements on state and local governments.

In response to *Boerne*, Congress considered new legislation, the Religious Liberty Protection Act (RLPA). Grounded primarily on the Constitution's Spending and Commerce Clauses, RLPA would have reimposed RFRA's compelling interest test on state and local laws and practices if they substantially burdened a person's religious exercise in a program or activity receiving federal financial assistance or if the substantial burden affected interstate commerce.[61] The House of Representatives passed a version of RLPA in 1999, but it did not become law. Instead, Congress later enacted a more limited statute, the Religious Land Use and Institutionalized Persons Act of 2000 (RLUIPA), which applies only to land use regulations and to regulations affecting institutionalized persons, including prisoners.[62] Like

60. Notably, *Gonzales* involved a claim similar to that addressed in *Smith* itself—the request for a religious exemption to permit the sacramental use of an otherwise illegal drug—and the Court ruled unanimously in favor of the claimant.

61. *See* H.R. 1691, 106th Cong. § 2(a) (1999).

62. 42 U.S.C. §§ 2000cc to 2000cc–5 (2006).

the broader RLPA proposal, RLUIPA relies especially on the Spending and Commerce Clauses in extending its requirements to state and local governments. The Act raises significant issues of federalism, but it so far has survived—or avoided—constitutional challenges addressing these concerns.[63]

In their own response to *Boerne*, some state legislatures have adopted RFRA-like statutes. Others are considering such legislation. State statutes, governing the states' own laws and practices, obviously present no federalism concerns, although they may raise other issues, including issues of state constitutional law.

In terms of federal constitutional law, the most significant issue presented by the state statutes is whether statutes of this sort, designed to "accommodate" the exercise of religion, in fact confer an impermissible benefit on religion and thereby violate the Establishment Clause. The federal statutes, RFRA and RLUIPA, present the same Establishment Clause question. Speaking to this issue in *Boerne*, but only for himself, Justice Stevens filed a brief concurrence contending that RFRA not only exceeded the power of Congress under Section 5 of the Fourteenth Amendment, but also violated the Establishment Clause.[64] More recently, by contrast,

63. *See*, *e.g.*, Cutter v. Wilkinson, 544 U.S. 709, 718 n.7 (2005) (noting, but not reaching, the argument that RLUIPA exceeds the power of Congress under the Spending and Commerce Clauses).

64. *Boerne*, 521 U.S. at 536–37 (Stevens, J., concurring).

in *Cutter v. Wilkinson*,[65] the Supreme Court unanimously rejected an Establishment Clause challenge to RLUIPA's recognition of prisoners' claims. *Cutter* and other precedents likewise suggest that the Establishment Clause probably does not threaten RLUIPA's other provisions, RFRA, or RFRA's state-law counterparts. We will return to this issue in the next chapter, when we address the concept of accommodation.

Constitutional Values and the Free Exercise Clause

There is deep and continuing controversy concerning the meaning of the Free Exercise Clause and the constitutional values it should be read to protect. The Supreme Court's contemporary doctrine confines itself largely to nondiscrimination and formal religious equality, and even these minimal standards do not always extend to indirect burdens. Apart from the Free Exercise Clause, free speech doctrine provides important additional protection, but it, too, focuses mainly on nondiscrimination and formal equality—in protecting private religious speech from discriminatory treatment. The recent legislative enactments protect religious conduct from some nondiscriminatory burdens, but the rights they confer are merely statutory. These statutory rights are significant and valuable, but they are subject to legislative repeal or modification, as

65.   544 U.S. 709 (2005).

well as constitutional limitations and potential invalidation, as *Boerne* makes clear. As for the Free Exercise Clause itself, one can argue that the Supreme Court's contemporary doctrine is inadequate and that the Court should give greater weight to religious voluntarism and other constitutional values. This argument might someday prevail, but it appears that a solid majority of the Court supports the current approach, and there is no indication that any major doctrinal change is in the offing.

Chapter 6

Interpreting the Establishment Clause

Like the Free Exercise Clause, the Establishment Clause was originally directed to Congress but today extends to the states as well. Its sparse text states that "Congress"—now understood to include the government generally—"shall make no law respecting an establishment of religion." These few words have given rise to a complex body of constitutional doctrine. We will examine the specifics in due course, but it is helpful to begin by briefly revisiting some of the basic concepts and principles that were introduced in Chapter 4.

To a large extent, the Establishment Clause has been interpreted to mirror the Free Exercise Clause. Thus, just as the Free Exercise Clause prevents the government from mistreating religion through the imposition of impermissible burdens, the Establishment Clause prohibits the government from advantaging religion through the conferral of impermissible benefits. It is important to remember that the constitutional definition of religion remains an open question under each clause. At least for purposes of the Establishment Clause, however, a broad definition is unlikely, and we can assume that religion probably is confined to beliefs and practices that are conventionally religious, which generally means theistic in nature. On this assumption, the Clause forbids impermissible benefits to religion in its conventional sense, and we are left to determine what counts as an impermissible benefit.

We will focus primarily on the question of when a benefit to religion is "impermissible." As noted in Chapter 4, however, a preliminary question is whether there is an Establishment Clause "benefit" at all. Unlike the comparable issue of constitutionally cognizable burdens under the Free Exercise Clause, this usually is not a difficult issue, and, indeed, the Court rarely discusses it as such. Generally speaking, when the government promotes or assists religion in any way, whether by discriminatory or nondiscriminatory means, it has conferred a benefit that passes this preliminary constitutional threshold. There is a contrary argument, however, when the government is removing what would otherwise be a legal burden on religion, even when, in so doing, the government is discriminating in religion's favor. This argument would arise, for example, in the defense of a religious exemption to an otherwise general prohibition on the use of peyote. In this type of situation, one can argue that the religious exemption conforms to Free Exercise values and therefore should not be seen as a "benefit" to religion under the Establishment Clause. We will return to this issue later, when we discuss the concept of "accommodation." For now, suffice it to say that this argument is plausible only if the government is providing relief from what would otherwise qualify as a direct or indirect burden on the exercise of religion, as discussed in Chapter 5. Outside the context of accommodation, virtually any assistance to religion can be seen as a benefit under the Establishment Clause. The critical question is whether the benefit is impermissible.

This question is not easy, and the appropriate answer in any given context is unavoidably value-laden. Indeed, the inquiry potentially implicates each of the six constitutional values or groups of values that were outlined in Chapter 3. The first three values should be familiar by now, because they were emphasized in Chapter 5, concerning the Free Exercise Clause. These values are important to the Establishment Clause as well. Thus, the Establishment Clause can be read, first, to disfavor governmental benefits that jeopardize religious voluntarism, for example, by inducing individuals to modify their religious beliefs or practices in order to qualify. Second, the Clause might be seen to protect the religious identity of dissenters, whether religious or irreligious, whose sense of self can be threatened when the government promotes or endorses religious beliefs they do not share. Third, religious equality, whether understood in a formal or more substantive sense, is obviously an important constitutional value—no less so here, in the context of legal benefits, than in the Free Exercise context of legal burdens.

The remaining constitutional values, although relevant in some respects to the Free Exercise Clause, are more often linked especially to the Establishment Clause. These values relate less to individual rights than to structural, institutional, or cultural considerations. Thus, the fourth set of constitutional values are the political values of promoting a religiously inclusive political community and protecting the government from improper religious involvement. When the conferral of benefits denigrates the religious identity of dissenters, for example, it might also create religious divisiveness that could threaten the unity of the political community itself. The fifth set of values are religious values, protecting religion from government and protecting the autonomy of religious institutions, values that can be impaired when governmental benefits have the perverse effect of compromising the vitality of religion and the independence of the organizations that promote it. The sixth and final value, preserving traditional governmental practices, acts as a potential counterweight in the Establishment Clause context. This value might support the constitutionality of certain traditional practices—for example, our national motto, "In God We Trust"—that appear to benefit religion in a way that might otherwise be impermissible.

In the course of this chapter, we will see how the interpretation, implementation, and weighing of these various constitutional values have influenced the development of the Supreme Court's Establishment Clause doctrine. In recent years, the Court's decisionmaking under the Establishment Clause, like its decisionmaking under the Free Exercise Clause, has emphasized the value of religious equality and has increasingly understood that value in formal rather than substantive terms. The other values have not disappeared from view, however, and the Court's Establishment Clause doctrine is considerably more complex than a simple prohibition on formal or deliberate discrimination.

In our attempt to elucidate the Supreme Court's decisionmaking, we will begin by highlighting the basic and important distinction between discriminatory and nondiscriminatory benefits to religion. We then will discuss the broad framework of the Court's Establishment Clause doctrine, examining the general constitutional tests and concepts that the Court has invoked. These include the three-part test of *Lemon v. Kurtzman*,[1] the endorsement test, a coercion test, and the concepts of tradition and accommodation. With this general framework in mind, the remainder of the chapter will turn to each of several, more specific areas of concern: religion and the public schools; religious symbolism in other public contexts; and public aid to religious schools, organizations, and individuals.

Discriminatory and Nondiscriminatory Benefits to Religion

Just as the Free Exercise Clause generally forbids discriminatory burdens on the exercise of religion, so, too, does the Establishment Clause generally forbid discriminatory benefits to religion, at least if

1.   403 U.S. 602 (1971).

the discrimination amounts to formal or deliberate discrimination in religion's favor. As we will see shortly, this prohibition is implemented through general constitutional tests requiring a secular, nonreligious purpose for lawmaking and forbidding governmental action that is adopted precisely for the purpose of promoting or endorsing religion. The prohibition also is reflected in the Court's specific rulings, including numerous decisions invalidating the deliberate and discriminatory promotion of religion over irreligion in the public schools, for example, through the schools' sponsorship of prayer or other religious practices. As explained in Chapter 4, the Establishment Clause prohibition on discriminatory benefits is all but absolute if the discrimination is sectarian, favoring one religion over another. Nonsectarian discrimination, favoring religion generally over irreligion, is usually unconstitutional as well, although it appears that there is a narrow exception for certain governmental practices that are traditional. Apart from this tradition-based exception, however, the prohibition on discriminatory benefits is broadly applied, and it is a well-established feature of the Court's doctrine. This prohibition obviously furthers formal religious equality. At the same time, it generally tends to promote substantive religious equality and other constitutional values as well.

The Court's general doctrinal tests imply that the Establishment Clause is concerned not only with deliberately discriminatory benefits, but also with other benefits to religion. These tests, for example, speak not only about the government's purposes, but also about the "primary effect" of its actions and possible impressions of governmental endorsement. They also speak about the risk of entanglement between religion and government. In the past, these sorts of considerations led to the invalidation of various programs of financial aid that did not formally discriminate in religion's favor. More recent decisions, however, have abandoned much of the reasoning and some of the holdings of these prior cases. According to the current Supreme Court, just as formal discrimination generally leads to invalidation, the absence of such discrimination generally is sufficient to satisfy the Establishment Clause. This position further elevates the value of formal equality, but, as we will see, it may jeopardize other constitutional values. Even so, these other values have not been entirely abandoned, and, indeed, some types of nondiscriminatory benefits to religion are still regarded as unconstitutional.

General Doctrinal Tests and Concepts

Remarkably enough, the current Supreme Court simultaneously recognizes three general Establishment Clause tests, each with different elements: the *Lemon* test, the endorsement test, and a coercion test. In addition, the Court's doctrine recognizes or considers two other general factors or concepts—tradition and accommodation—that are not explicit in any of the three general tests. This section will attempt to explain the development and content of these tests and concepts, their current significance, their relationship to each other, and their linkage to constitutional values.

The final concept, that of accommodation, connects this chapter to the last one by addressing the relationship between the Establishment Clause and the Free Exercise Clause. In particular, it confronts the question of when the Establishment Clause permits the government to advance Free Exercise values. Accommodation is important not only for its general doctrinal significance, but also as a specialized and complicated field of Establishment Clause doctrine in its own right. As a result, accommodation will require more substantial elaboration than the other tests and concepts discussed in this section.

Lemon

In its 1947 decision in *Everson v. Board of Education*,[2] the Supreme Court announced a broad and strict interpretation of the Establishment Clause. The Court's interpretation appeared to require not merely formal equality between and among religions and between religion and irreligion, nor even substantive equality, but also a separation of religion and government. Quoting Thomas Jefferson, the Court declared that "the clause against establishment of religion by law was intended to erect 'a wall of separation between church and State.'"[3] In

2. 330 U.S. 1 (1947).

3. *Id.* at 16.

the years following *Everson*, the Court articulated doctrinal standards that were designed to implement this philosophy. In 1971, the Court consolidated these standards in *Lemon v. Kurtzman*[4] by announcing a general, three-pronged test for Establishment Clause cases. To survive judicial scrutiny, the Court stated, a statute (or other governmental action) must satisfy each of three requirements: "First, the statute must have a secular legislative purpose; second, its principal or primary effect must be one that neither advances nor inhibits religion . . .; finally, the statute must not foster 'an excessive governmental entanglement with religion.' "[5]

Since 1971, the Supreme Court has applied the *Lemon* test in a wide variety of Establishment Clause cases. In recent years, the test has been harshly criticized by various justices, but the Court nonetheless continues to use it, albeit less often than in the past and sometimes in modified form. In a 2000 school prayer case, for example, and again in a 2005 decision concerning public displays of the Ten Commandments, a majority—much to the chagrin of the dissenting justices—cited the *Lemon* test and relied upon its first prong in finding constitutional violations.[6] Likewise, the Court has utilized the *Lemon* factors in recent financial aid cases even

4.   403 U.S. 602 (1971).

5.   *Id.* at 612–13.

6.   Santa Fe Indep. Sch. Dist. v. Doe, 530 U.S. 290, 314–16 (2000); McCreary County v. ACLU of Ky., 545 U.S. 844, 859–74 (2005).

as its decisions have substantially relaxed the Establishment Clause barriers in that context. Thus, the Court has stated that it "continue[s] to ask whether the government acted with the purpose of advancing or inhibiting religion" and "continue[s] to explore whether the aid has the 'effect' of advancing or inhibiting religion."[7] At least in the financial aid context, however, the Court has indicated that it no longer regards entanglement as a separate prong, treating it instead as one aspect of the effect inquiry and thereby weakening its doctrinal significance.[8]

We need not dwell long on the Court's references to "inhibiting religion." Here and in other statements of doctrine, the Supreme Court has included language that can be read to suggest that the Establishment Clause not only precludes certain benefits to religion, but also certain disadvantages. This language may capture an appropriate sense of governmental neutrality, but it is doctrinally confusing, because the Establishment Clause, as such, is better reserved for cases involving governmental attempts to benefit religion. If the government is hindering or burdening religion, the more appropriate analysis is that of the Free Exercise Clause. Indeed, despite its references to "inhibiting religion," the Supreme Court has never relied upon this language to protect religion from a governmentally imposed disadvantage. For all practical purposes, then, we can ignore this and similar doctrinal language and limit the

7. Agostini v. Felton, 521 U.S. 203, 222–23 (1997).

8. *See id.* at 232–33.

Court's Establishment Clause tests to governmental attempts to benefit religion.[9] So understood, the *Lemon* test precludes governmental action that has the non-secular purpose of advancing religion (either one religion or religion generally) or the primary effect of so doing. Whether separately or as a part of the effect prong, the test also precludes benefits that create an excessive entanglement between religion and government.

The first prong of *Lemon*, precluding the government from acting with the purpose of advancing religion, essentially embodies a requirement of formal equality between and among religions and between religion and irreligion. This prong prevents the government from purposefully discriminating in favor of religion (either one religion or religion generally) through the award of deliberately discriminatory benefits. The second prong, focusing on the actual effect of the governmental action, may reflect a more substantive understanding of religious equality, one that might be informed by religious voluntarism and other values. The entanglement inquiry suggests a concern for institutional separation, a concern that may point to structural constitutional values, both political and religious. In any event, the very existence of the effect and entanglement elements of the *Lemon* test, whatever

9. This is not to deny that in the examination of governmentally conferred benefits, the Court might appropriately consider the risks that the benefits might pose for the vitality of religion and of religious institutions. To this extent, unintended disadvantages to religion may play a role in the Court's Establishment Clause analysis.

their precise meanings, clearly implies that formal equality is not always sufficient under the Establishment Clause.

Endorsement

In 1984, in her influential concurring opinion in *Lynch v. Donnelly*,[10] Justice O'Connor proposed a "clarification" of *Lemon* that has since been embraced by the Court as a separate doctrinal tool. O'Connor argued that *Lemon* should be understood to forbid the government from endorsing religion, either deliberately or in effect, and that the first two prongs of *Lemon* should be modified accordingly.[11] Under the modified test, the government violates the Establishment Clause if it intends to communicate a message that endorses religion (either one religion or religion generally) or if, whatever the government's intention, its action has the effect of communicating such a message. (The endorsement test does not separately address the issue of entanglement.)

As a practical matter, the modified first prong adds little to the original *Lemon* formulation, because it is difficult to find purposeful advancement of religion without purposeful endorsement, and vice versa. The second prong of the endorsement test, however, suggests a potentially important shift

10.   465 U.S. 668, 687–94 (1984) (O'Connor, J., concurring).

11.   In fact, Justice O'Connor interpreted *Lemon* to preclude not only governmental "endorsement" of religion, but also governmental "disapproval." Like the Court's references to "inhibiting religion," however, this part of O'Connor's reformulation is doctrinally confusing and, as a practical matter, it is largely inconsequential.

of focus. This prong examines the effect of the challenged governmental action symbolically, looking in particular at its objective meaning. Thus, the Court is to determine whether a "reasonable observer" or an "objective observer," properly informed of the relevant history and context, would find in the government's action a message that endorses religion. Even if, in the language of *Lemon*, governmental action might have the primary effect of advancing religion, it is not unconstitutional under the second prong of the endorsement test unless it carries this impermissible message. Conversely, it is at least possible that governmental action could convey a message of governmental endorsement even if it does not appreciably advance religion, at least not in any tangible way. The modified second prong requires qualitative and sensitive judgments about symbolic meaning, whereas the original second prong arguably contemplates a more quantitative inquiry into the nature and degree of concrete legal benefits.

In various Establishment Clause settings, the Supreme Court has adopted and utilized one or both prongs of Justice O'Connor's endorsement reformulation, often in conjunction with the original *Lemon* test. Indeed, the Court recently has extended the endorsement test's "reasonable observer" or "objective observer" perspective—a concept originally linked to the second prong of the endorsement analysis—by invoking it to help inform the first prong of the *Lemon* and endorsement tests as well. As the Court explained, this is a fitting perspective because the investigation of governmental purpose is an objective inquiry, not a search for hidden or secret motivations.[12]

As with *Lemon* itself, the endorsement test has encountered significant opposition among the justices, but it has been and remains a viable part of the Court's doctrine. As we will discuss later, the endorsement test has been especially important in the context of religious symbolism, including public displays that include religious elements. More broadly, it stands today as a general standard that supplements and complements the conventional *Lemon* inquiry.[13]

To some extent, the endorsement test reflects the same constitutional values as those of *Lemon* itself. Thus, its first prong promotes formal religious equality, and its second prong may tend to serve substantive equality and perhaps religious voluntarism. The test's specific focus on governmental messages of endorsement, however, gives special attention to two other values: respecting the religious identity of dissenting citizens and promoting a religiously inclusive political community. Governmental endorsements of religion, without more, may have little or no influence on religious beliefs and practices and therefore may not meaningfully impair religious voluntarism. But they are quite likely

12. *See* McCreary County v. ACLU of Ky., 545 U.S. 844, 861–63 (2005).

13. *See, e.g.,* County of Allegheny v. ACLU, 492 U.S. 573, 592–94 (1989); Santa Fe Indep. Sch. Dist. v. Doe, 530 U.S. 290, 301–10 (2000); Zelman v. Simmons–Harris, 536 U.S. 639, 654–55 (2002).

to affront and alienate dissenting citizens, whether religious or irreligious, who are conspicuously excluded from the government's symbolic favor. As Justice O'Connor wrote in her *Lynch* concurrence, "Endorsement sends a message to nonadherents that they are outsiders, not full members of the political community...."[14] As to these dissenters, the government's action, endorsing religious beliefs they do not share, may constitute not only an insult, but also a psychological assault on the core of their self-identity. By denigrating the dissenters' identity, moreover, the governmental action is likely to create resentment and religious divisiveness that could threaten the unity of the political community itself.[15]

Coercion

Critics of *Lemon* and of the endorsement test long have argued that those tests are too restrictive. They contend that the government should have greater leeway to support religion and to do so deliberately, as long as the support is nonsectarian, not favoring any particular religion over others. According to one version of this argument, the only appropriate limit on nonsectarian support is a test of coercion. Under such a test, governmental action would not violate the Establishment Clause unless it coerced dissenting citizens. Otherwise, the gov-

14. *Lynch*, 465 U.S. at 688 (O'Connor, J., concurring).

15. For an elaboration of these themes, see Daniel O. Conkle, *Toward a General Theory of the Establishment Clause*, 82 Nw. U. L. Rev. 1113, 1172–79 (1988).

ernment would be perfectly free to advance or endorse religion over irreligion.

The proper inquiry under a coercion test is subject to debate, but it might mirror the inquiry into substantial burdens on the exercise of religion, as discussed in Chapter 5. As we learned in that chapter, the Free Exercise Clause protects against direct and indirect burdens on the exercise of religion, at least if the burdens are both substantial and discriminatory. In like fashion, when the government is discriminating in religion's favor, the Establishment Clause might protect dissenters from direct and indirect coercive pressure on their desire *not* to engage in religious conduct. Under this analysis, governmental action would violate the Establishment Clause either if it required individuals to engage in religious conduct or if it placed dissenters on the horns of a decisional dilemma, for example, by offering financial or other benefits only to those who were willing to acquiesce in the conduct. Indirect coercion, at least, is a matter of degree. As in the analogous Free Exercise context, however, a finding of illicit coercion presumably would be appropriate if the governmental action exerted substantial pressure on the dissenters' decisionmaking process.

Whatever its precise meaning, the coercion test is linked specifically and narrowly to the value of religious voluntarism. Standing alone, it reads the Establishment Clause to disfavor nonsectarian benefits to religion only if the governmental action substantially impedes the freedom of individuals to make and implement religious choices, including especially the choice not to participate in religious conduct. Clearly, such a serious intrusion on religious voluntarism should be seen as a core violation of the Establishment Clause. But the coercion test largely ignores other constitutional values. In the absence of coercion, it does not require the government to respect the self-identity of dissenters. Nor does it honor the value of religious equality, either formal or substantive, insofar as that value calls for equality between religion and irreligion. It also gives very little weight to structural values, including those that protect the government and the political community and those that protect religion and religious institutions.

Despite its limited perspective, an approach emphasizing coercion had attracted considerable support on the Supreme Court by the late 1980s, and, in 1992, there was speculation that a majority might move in this direction in *Lee v. Weisman*.[16] In fact, the Court in *Weisman* did utilize a coercion analysis of sorts, but, over the vigorous dissent of four justices, the Court nonetheless concluded that it was unconstitutional for a public school to sponsor a clergy-led, nonsectarian prayer at a graduation ceremony. Unlike the dissenting justices, the Court took an extremely broad view of illicit governmental coercion. Noting the "subtle coercive pressure" of the public school environment and the role of "public pressure, as well as peer pressure," the Court found that the school had placed object-

16.   505 U.S. 577 (1992).

ing students in an "untenable position" of "indirect coercion." This coercion did not necessarily induce objecting students to actively join the prayer, even silently. But it did subject them to "pressure, though subtle and indirect," to "participate" in a more passive way. Thus, they felt obliged to attend the ceremony despite their objection, and, once there, they felt obliged to quietly acquiesce in the prayer, giving others the impression that they either were joining or approving it.[17] This analysis suggests that it is unconstitutional for the government to coerce individuals, even by indirect and subtle means, into a situation that creates the *appearance* that they are participating in or approving religious conduct to which they actually object. Notably, the Court in *Weisman* explicitly declined to reconsider *Lemon*, and its overall analysis—including its capacious understanding of coercion—suggested a continuing reliance on elements of the *Lemon* and endorsement approaches.[18]

In the wake of *Weisman*, coercion has become a more explicit part of the Supreme Court's Establishment Clause doctrine, but not as a replacement for the Court's other tests. Instead, the coercion test—in the broad form expounded in *Weisman*— has become yet another doctrinal tool, one that stands alongside *Lemon* and the endorsement test. Thus, in a 2000 school prayer decision, the Court used all three tests, including a *Weisman*-like anal-

17. *See id.* at 590–99.

18. *See* Daniel O. Conkle, Lemon *Lives*, 43 Case W. Res. L. Rev. 865 (1993).

ysis of coercion, in the course of invalidating a public school policy that promoted student-led prayers before high school football games.[19] In reality, however, the coercion test is largely superfluous. Whenever there is coercion favoring religion, however subtle and indirect, there also is advancement or endorsement in violation of the Court's other Establishment Clause tests. As a matter of current doctrine, that advancement or endorsement generally is enough, in itself, to render the governmental action unconstitutional, meaning that coercion is not an essential element of an Establishment Clause claim.[20] Accordingly, as long as *Lemon* and the endorsement test are applicable, it seems that the presence of coercion simply provides an additional basis for finding a constitutional violation and, perhaps, for finding the violation especially egregious. (As the next subsection indicates, there appears to be an implicit exception to *Lemon* and the endorsement test, an exception based on tradition. In the context of that limited exception, the presence or absence of coercion may have greater relevance.)

19. Santa Fe Indep. Sch. Dist. v. Doe, 530 U.S. 290 (2000).

20. In *Van Orden v. Perry*, 545 U.S. 677 (2005), a Ten Commandments case to which we will return later, a four-justice plurality adopted a lenient approach, rejecting the *Lemon* test (and implicitly the endorsement test) in the context of "passive" religious symbolism outside the public school context, in part precisely because such symbolism is passive as opposed to coercive. *See id.* at 686–92 (plurality opinion). This opinion arguably moves in the direction of making coercion an essential element of an Establishment Clause claim, but the scope of the opinion is limited, and, in any event, it did not command majority support.

Tradition

Although the *Lemon* and endorsement tests clearly dominate the Supreme Court's doctrine, the Court has indicated that the Establishment Clause permits some governmental practices that would appear to violate these tests. In its 1983 decision in *Marsh v. Chambers*,[21] for example, the Court upheld the practice of legislative prayer by publicly paid chaplains. At that time, *Lemon* was the governing Establishment Clause test, the endorsement test having not yet arisen as a separate doctrinal tool. Under any serious application of *Lemon*, however, it is difficult to deny that legislative prayer has both the purpose and effect of advancing religion. The practice might also be seen as a quintessential entanglement of religion and government. Perhaps not surprisingly, therefore, the Court in *Marsh* made no pretense of applying the *Lemon* test, which it ignored altogether. Instead, the Court emphasized that legislative prayer goes back to the First Congress and is such a longstanding tradition that it is "part of the fabric of our society."[22]

In dicta in other cases, the Court likewise has approved other traditional practices that, by every indication, not only advance and endorse religion, but do so deliberately. It has cited with approval, for example, each of the following: presidential Thanksgiving proclamations that, since the time of George Washington, have included religious references and appeals; the Supreme Court's own open-

21. 463 U.S. 783 (1983).

22. *Id.* at 792.

ing cry, "God Save the United States and this Honorable Court," which dates to the tenure of Chief Justice John Marshall; our national motto, "In God We Trust," which became official in 1956, and the inclusion of this phrase on our money, a practice that began in the 1800s and that has extended to all currency since the 1950s; and the statutorily prescribed language, "one Nation under God," which has been part of the Pledge of Allegiance since 1954.[23]

If a governmental practice dates back to the founding, one might contend, as did the Court in *Marsh*, that its constitutionality is supported not only by tradition, but also by the original understanding of the First Amendment.[24] As noted in Chapter 2, however, this sort of selective reliance on the original understanding is problematic and unpersuasive. Using an alternative argument, the Court sometimes has implied that the traditional practices it approves actually can satisfy *Lemon* and the endorsement test because they merely "acknowledge" or "recognize" religion without advancing or endorsing it. Going one step further, some justices have suggested that these practices, despite their references and appeals to God, have lost their religious meaning over time and now serve symbolic purposes that are secular in nature.[25] These various

23. *See, e.g.*, Lynch v. Donnelly, 465 U.S. 668, 674–78 (1984).

24. In *Marsh*, the Court emphasized that the First Congress, the same Congress that framed the First Amendment, specifically approved the practice of legislative prayer.

25. *See, e.g.*, *Lynch*, 465 U.S. at 716–17 (Brennan, J., dissenting).

arguments may or may not be persuasive, but a more straightforward explanation is available, one that does not ignore the religious character of these practices and that is willing to concede that they do promote religion. This explanation relies directly on tradition as a source of constitutional meaning, and it identifies what amounts to a "tradition" exception to the *Lemon* and endorsement tests.

The contours of this implicit exception are quite uncertain, in part because the Supreme Court has been reluctant to formally recognize its existence. Even so, it appears that the exception generally requires that three criteria be satisfied. First, the governmental practice must represent a widely accepted and longstanding American tradition. The tradition need not date back to the founding, but the deeper and the older it is, the stronger the case for upholding it. Second, the government's promotion of religion must be nonsectarian, not favoring any particular religion over others.[26] And third, the governmental support for religion must be primarily and fundamentally symbolic, rather than tangible or coercive. Thus, it must not involve significant financial support for religion or religious institutions, and it must not improperly coerce dissenting citizens. The question of improper coercion leads back to some form of the coercion test, giving that inquiry significance in this context.

26. Even general references to "God," including "In God We Trust" and "one Nation under God," may not embrace all religions. But they are treated as nonsectarian because they do not promote any particular religion and because they are broadly inclusive of various religious perspectives.

There may be other considerations as well, beyond these three criteria. For example, the government's promotion of a general religious reference or declaration may be more acceptable than its promotion of a prayer or other act of religious worship. If so, the exception might permit the Supreme Court, despite its school prayer rulings, to approve school-sponsored recitations of the Pledge of Allegiance, complete with its "under God" language. The Court confronted—but avoided—this Establishment Clause issue in its 2004 decision in *Elk Grove Unified School District v. Newdow*,[27] ruling that the question was not justiciable because the challenger (a parent with limited and disputed custodial rights) lacked "prudential standing" to bring the case in federal court. But three justices would have reached the merits, and each would have rejected the Establishment Clause claim. Two of them, Chief Justice Rehnquist and Justice O'Connor, cited reasons generally consistent with an implicit exception along the lines we have discussed.[28]

The "under God" language in the Pledge of Allegiance dates back to 1954, and the religious reference is nonsectarian, but what about the exception's third condition, in particular, the requirement that there be no improper coercion? In *West Virginia State Board of Education v. Bar-*

27.   542 U.S. 1 (2004).

28.   *See id.* at 25–33 (Rehnquist, C.J., concurring in the judgment); *id.* at 33–45 (O'Connor, J., concurring in the judgment). Justice Thomas was the third justice, but he urged a broader modification of Establishment Clause doctrine. *See id.* at 45–54 (Thomas, J., concurring in the judgment).

nette,[29] the Supreme Court held that public schools cannot directly compel objecting students to recite the Pledge. But in the face of an Establishment Clause challenge, this freedom from direct coercion might or might not be sufficient. The Court's school prayer decisions make it clear that the risk of indirect and subtle coercion, as discussed in *Lee v. Weisman*, is reason enough to reject a tradition-based exception for school-sponsored nonsectarian prayer in the public school setting, even if the prayer is formally voluntary. But as Chief Justice Rehnquist and Justice O'Connor emphasized in *Newdow*, the Pledge of Allegiance is not a prayer or religious exercise. It is a patriotic exercise that includes a brief and general religious reference or declaration.[30] Moreover, a student who objects only to the "under God" language is free to remain silent during that portion of the Pledge. These factors mitigate the concern about coercion, reducing the threat to religious voluntarism, and perhaps the weight of tradition can overcome the lingering potential for indirect and subtle coercion. If so, then it may be enough that students cannot be directly or substantially coerced to actively join the recitation. In any event, the Pledge of Allegiance issue tests the scope of the implicit exception, and, in light of the Court's justiciability ruling in

29. 319 U.S. 624 (1943).

30. *See Newdow*, 542 U.S. at 31 (Rehnquist, C.J., concurring in the judgment); *id.* at 39–43 (O'Connor, J., concurring in the judgment).

Newdow, the Establishment Clause question remains open.

Whatever the precise scope of the implicit exception and however the Supreme Court might describe its reasoning, it seems that tradition informs the Court's doctrine by acting as a partial counterweight to other constitutional values.[31] As long as the exception does not permit any serious coercion, it does not meaningfully impair religious voluntarism. It does limit the value of religious equality in this context, however, to equality between and among religions, not between religion and irreligion. It likewise permits governmental action that disrespects the religious identity of dissenting citizens and that, as a result, might undermine the religious inclusiveness of the political community. Even so, these harms are lessened by the intangible and non-coercive character of the government's action, and tradition is a competing value that prop-

31. Beyond the implicit exception as such, tradition sometimes may lead the Court to apply its conventional doctrine less strictly than usual. For possible examples, see McGowan v. Maryland, 366 U.S. 420, 431–53 (1961) (upholding traditional Sunday closing laws, despite their religious origins, on the ground that they no longer have either the purpose or effect of aiding religion); Walz v. Tax Comm'n, 397 U.S. 664, 672–80 (1970) (finding that the extension of nonprofit tax-exempt status to religious organizations does not sponsor or advance religion and emphasizing that this longstanding governmental practice "is not something to be lightly cast aside"); Lynch v. Donnelly, 465 U.S. 668, 675–76, 678–85 (1984) (finding no violation of *Lemon* in a city's inclusion of a nativity scene in a Christmas display, but only after noting with approval the government's traditional recognition of both Christmas and Thanksgiving as holidays with religious significance).

erly is relevant to constitutional interpretation. Moreover, the very fact that the practices reflect traditional policies, not new ones, might further mitigate the impairment of other constitutional values. In particular, dissenters might be somewhat more willing to accept the practices as imbedded features of the status quo, not contemporary statements of disrespect, and this in turn might reduce the likelihood of their alienation from the political community.[32]

Accommodation

The term "accommodation" has more than one meaning. For instance, it sometimes is used as a generic description for relaxed interpretations of the Establishment Clause, interpretations permitting the government to accommodate or even favor religion in various contexts. As used here, by contrast, the term has a more specific meaning, one that describes the government's power to accommodate not religion, but *religious freedom*. More specifically, it describes the extent to which the Establishment Clause, informed by the Free Exercise Clause, permits the government to grant special protection to the exercise of religion by exempting religious conduct from legal burdens that would otherwise be applicable. This special protection might appear to advance and endorse religion—and to do so deliberately—in violation of the *Lemon* and endorsement tests. As a result, one might think of

32. For a more elaborate and somewhat different argument concerning the role of tradition under the Establishment Clause, see Conkle, *supra* note 15, at 1183–87.

accommodation, like tradition, as an implicit exception to the Supreme Court's usual doctrinal tests. In reality, however, when accommodation is permitted, there is no benefit to religion that is constitutionally cognizable under the Establishment Clause. The point is subtle but important: it is religious freedom, not religion as such, that the government is advancing and endorsing. Thus, it is better to think of accommodation as religion-specific governmental action that facilitates and prefers the exercise of religion, but that does so in a manner that legitimately satisfies the Court's conventional Establishment Clause doctrine.

The Religion Clauses do not work at cross-purposes. At the very least, therefore, the concept of accommodation means that the government does not violate the Establishment Clause when it takes action that is constitutionally required by the Free Exercise Clause. Under current doctrine, the Free Exercise Clause generally does not protect religious conduct from nondiscriminatory burdens. Accordingly, it generally does not require religion-specific remedial action that would even arguably implicate the Establishment Clause. Prior to *Employment Division v. Smith*,[33] by contrast, the Free Exercise Clause sometimes required the government to exempt religious conduct from substantial burdens, even when the burdens resulted from nondiscriminatory, generally applicable laws. One could argue that these constitutionally required exemptions— for religious conduct and religious conduct alone—

33. 494 U.S. 872 (1990).

constituted benefits to religion in violation of the Establishment Clause. Reading the Religion Clauses together, however, the Supreme Court properly rejected that argument, finding that the removal of a Free Exercise burden does not amount to an Establishment Clause benefit. Even today, this reasoning still applies to the limited extent, if any, that the Free Exercise Clause continues to provide protection from nondiscriminatory burdens and therefore requires preferential treatment for religious conduct.

Even when the accommodation of religious conduct is not required by the Free Exercise Clause, it is permissible, within limits, in the discretion of the government. In *Smith*, the Court broadly rejected the notion of constitutionally required accommodation. As we saw in Chapter 5, this restrictive interpretation of the Free Exercise Clause elevates the value of formal religious equality and gives only limited weight to other constitutional values. Even as the Court in *Smith* resisted vigorous judicial enforcement of the Free Exercise Clause, however, it emphasized that values reflected in the Bill of Rights, including the Free Exercise Clause, are not "banished from the political process." It thus suggested that legislatures are free to protect religious voluntarism and other Free Exercise values—not as a matter of constitutional compulsion, but as a matter of legislative policy. In particular, the Court reaffirmed the permissibility of "nondiscriminatory religious-practice exemption[s]" from otherwise general laws and noted with approval, for example, that "a number of States have made an exception to their drug laws for sacramental peyote use."[34] Quite clearly, the Court did not regard the Establishment Clause as a barrier to such exemptions.

The Court in *Smith* spoke of state-law exemptions created by state legislative action, but the concept of permissible accommodation also applies to federal-law exemptions adopted by Congress. It likewise extends to state-law exemptions arising from state constitutional law. This is important because the courts of some states, interpreting state constitutional provisions protecting the free exercise of religion, have adhered to an approach along the lines of federal constitutional doctrine prior to *Smith*. Utilizing that approach as a matter of state constitutional law, state courts may call for religion-based exemptions from state laws that are otherwise nondiscriminatory and generally applicable.

Although state constitutional law is one source of permissible accommodation, the primary source is legislative action. Resting mainly in the hands of legislatures, permissible accommodation is hardly a perfect vehicle for protecting Free Exercise values. In the first place, unlike the case-by-case adjudication of courts, legislatures act through general enactments. At the time of enactment, a legislature might not be aware that a law will affect religious conduct in some future application. Obviously, if the legislature does not anticipate such a case, it will not consider the possibility of a religion-based exemption. Second, to the extent that legislatures do consider exemptions, they might well reject

34. *Id.* at 890.

them, especially if the exemptions would protect religious practices that are unconventional. As the Supreme Court conceded in *Smith*, "leaving accommodation to the political process" places minority religious practices "at a relative disadvantage,"[35] a prospect that threatens the value of substantive religious equality. Whatever its weaknesses, however, permissible accommodation is the only available vehicle for honoring Free Exercise values that the Court no longer protects as a matter of constitutional right. More specifically, permissible accommodation can provide religion-based exemptions that protect religious conduct from nondiscriminatory burdens—burdens that, after *Smith*, are largely immune from the Free Exercise Clause itself.

It is critical, therefore, to determine the legitimate scope of permissible accommodation and, in particular, to determine the limits that the Establishment Clause imposes in this context. One Establishment Clause limit is linked to *Lemon*'s concern about the institutional entanglement of religion and government. Thus, even if the government is attempting to protect the exercise of religion, it cannot adopt a religion-based exception to an otherwise applicable law if the exception amounts to a purposeful delegation of governmental power to a religious organization or group. For example, the government cannot protect the exercise of religion by granting churches the power to veto liquor licenses for nearby restaurants.[36] Apart from this prohibi-

35. *Id.*

36. *See* Larkin v. Grendel's Den, Inc., 459 U.S. 116 (1982); *see also* Board of Educ. of Kiryas Joel Village Sch. Dist. v. Grumet, 512 U.S. 687 (1994) (invalidating the creation of a

tion on improper delegation, the Establishment Clause limits in this area are imprecise and uncertain. Even so, it appears that legislative action (or state constitutional interpretation) must meet two basic requirements in order to qualify as permissible accommodation and therefore avoid Establishment Clause invalidation.

First, the religion-based exemption must be designed to provide relief from what would otherwise be a governmentally imposed, substantial burden on the exercise of religion. As discussed in Chapter 5, a substantial burden is a direct or indirect burden that dissuades or discourages the exercise of religion by exerting substantial coercive pressure on religious decisionmaking. In the context of permissible accommodation, the legislature (or state court interpreting the state's constitution) may have some leeway in assessing the substantiality of a burden, permitting it to address burdens that the Supreme Court might not regard as sufficiently substantial to be constitutionally cognizable under the Free Exercise Clause itself. But the burden must at least be one that the legislature (or state court) could reasonably characterize as substantial.[37] Otherwise, a religion-based exemption would be promoting religion, not religious freedom.

special public school district that was drawn to include only the members of a discrete community of Hasidic Jews).

37. *Cf.* Corporation of the Presiding Bishop v. Amos, 483 U.S. 327, 335–36 (1987) (suggesting that permissible accommodation legitimately can address "significant" burdens).

This requirement that permissible accommodation be designed to relieve a substantial burden helps explain the Supreme Court's competing results in two Establishment Clause cases, both decided in the late 1980s. In *Texas Monthly, Inc. v. Bullock*,[38] the Court invalidated a sales tax exemption for the sale of religious literature by religious organizations. Although the Court could not agree on an opinion, a majority of the justices concluded that this religion-based exemption violated the Establishment Clause. As part of its reasoning, the plurality opinion emphasized that the exemption was not designed to protect religious scruples or religious decisionmaking. Rather, the burden of the sales tax, at least for most religious organizations, was simply financial. The tax exemption therefore was not redressing a substantial burden on religious exercise, and it did not qualify as permissible accommodation.[39] Conversely, in *Corporation of the Presiding Bishop v. Amos*,[40] the Court approved, as

38. 489 U.S. 1 (1989).

39. A sales tax exemption extending more broadly, to religious and nonreligious literature alike, would be a different matter. Under the reasoning of the plurality in *Texas Monthly*, the broader exemption still would fall outside the zone of permissible accommodation, because it would not be redressing a substantial burden on religious exercise. But the benefit to religion might now be seen as nondiscriminatory, and it might therefore be approved under the basic standards of *Lemon* and the endorsement test. *Cf.* Walz v. Tax Comm'n, 397 U.S. 664 (1970) (approving a scheme of property tax exemptions that extended to religious organizations along with other nonprofit organizations).

40. 483 U.S. 327 (1987).

permissible accommodation, a religion-based exemption in Title VII of the Civil Rights Act of 1964. The Act generally prohibits religious discrimination in employment, but it exempts religious organizations so that they can make religion-based employment decisions, even for jobs without specifically religious duties. According to the Court, Congress permissibly concluded that without the exemption, the Act's prohibition would have substantially burdened the exercise of religion. In particular, it would have impaired the ability of religious organizations to define and carry out their religious missions by preventing them from making and implementing religious decisions in selecting organizational personnel. Unlike the exemption rejected in *Texas Monthly*, the exemption approved in *Amos* was designed to protect religiously informed conduct, that is, conduct that reflected decisions of religious conscience or religious doctrine.

A second requirement for permissible accommodation, as the Court suggested in *Smith*, is that the religion-based exemption must be "nondiscriminatory." This requirement does not prevent the government from preferring the exercise of religion over nonreligious conduct. As the Court wrote in *Amos*, "Where, as here, government acts with the proper purpose of lifting a regulation that burdens the exercise of religion, we see no reason to require that the exemption come packaged with benefits to secular entities."[41] Rather, the requirement of "nondiscriminatory" accommodation merely pre-

41. *Id.* at 338.

cludes discrimination between or among religions. This ban on sectarian discrimination, however, raises questions of its own. One important question relates to the critical issue of definition that the Supreme Court has yet to resolve: what qualifies as a religion for the purpose of defining religious exercise? If religion is given a broad definition for this purpose, one that includes deeply held moral beliefs of various sorts, it might be improperly "sectarian" to discriminate among "religions" by limiting an exemption to *conventional* religions. Under this sort of reasoning, for example, it might be unconstitutional to grant an exemption from compulsory military service to those who conscientiously object for reasons that are conventionally religious, but to deny the same treatment to others whose moral values lead them to the same ethical position.[42]

However religion is defined, moreover, different religions have different tenets and practices, meaning that an exemption designed to protect one form of religious exercise may help one religion but not another. An exemption for the religious use of peyote, for example, protects members of the Native American Church in their sacramental practice, but it does nothing to protect the Amish or Orthodox Jews from legal requirements that might impede

42. In *United States v. Seeger*, 380 U.S. 163 (1965), and *Welsh v. United States*, 398 U.S. 333 (1970), the Supreme Court avoided this constitutional issue by interpreting a statutory religious-objector provision expansively, permitting it to extend to objectors who were not conventionally religious. These cases are addressed in Chapter 4's discussion of the problem of defining religion.

their particular forms of religious exercise. Yet differential treatment in this general sense does not constitute improper sectarian discrimination; if it did, permissible accommodation for specific religious practices would be nearly impossible. Rather, the forbidden sectarian discrimination is present only when an exemption is not extended to all religions that face the same or comparable situations. The ban on sectarian discrimination certainly requires, for example, that the government extend an exemption for the religious use of peyote to all religions that use peyote in a manner comparable to the Native American Church.[43] Beyond this obvious point, however, the determination of sectarian discrimination is more difficult, and it requires the exercise of judgment. The governing principle appears to be this: accommodating one religious practice but not a similar one is improperly sectarian if, but only if, the distinction cannot reasonably be justified on the basis of the government's secular interests. For example, if the government exempts religious users of peyote from its drug laws, must it also exempt those who use marijuana or heroin for religious reasons? Perhaps, but probably not. The

43. If the government grants an exemption to a specific religious group, creating the risk of sectarian discrimination, it may be required to provide or authorize the exemption for other, similarly situated religious groups at the same time, rather than simply await the other groups' requests for their own exemptions. *Cf.* Board of Educ. of Kiryas Joel Village Sch. Dist. v. Grumet, 512 U.S. 687, 702–07 (1994) (invalidating the creation of a special public school district for a community of Hasidic Jews, based in part on a concern that other religious (and nonreligious) groups would not be treated in like fashion).

issue is whether the government's secular interests can reasonably justify its decision to exempt for peyote but not for the other drugs.

The question of reasonable justification itself requires a comparison of the two competing situations under an inquiry analogous to the "strict scrutiny" that governed *constitutional* claims for exemptions prior to *Smith*. As Justice Blackmun wrote in his unsuccessful defense of that constitutional regime, "Though the State must treat all religions equally, and not favor one over another, this obligation is fulfilled by the uniform application of the 'compelling interest' test to all free exercise claims, not by reaching uniform results as to all claims."[44] As to permissible accommodation, it seems that a modified version of Blackmun's argument remains valid: the government can grant one exemption but not another that is arguably similar as long as there is a distinction that is *reasonable* in terms of the relative strength of the government's secular interests and the relative harm to those interests that a religious exemption would cause. For example, granting a religious exemption for the use of marijuana or heroin, for which there are significant illegal markets and extensive nonreligious demand, might seriously undermine the government's anti-drug campaign in a way that a peyote exemption might not.[45]

44. Employment Div. v. Smith, 494 U.S. 872, 918 (1990) (Blackmun, J., dissenting) (emphasis omitted).

45. *See id.* at 916–19.

Permissible accommodation traditionally has taken the form of specific exemptions from particular laws. Congress exempts religious employers from particular provisions of Title VII, for instance, or states exempt the sacramental use of peyote from their criminal drug laws. As discussed at the end of Chapter 5, however, the Supreme Court's restrictive interpretation of the Free Exercise Clause recently has given rise to accommodation statutes of a different and quite remarkable sort. They include the Religious Freedom Restoration Act of 1993 (RFRA), the Religious Land Use and Institutionalized Persons Act of 2000 (RLUIPA), and comparable state statutes. These statutes demand strict scrutiny (at least of the variety applied by the Supreme Court in Free Exercise cases before *Smith*) for substantial burdens on the exercise of religion in a wide variety of governmental contexts. Because the statutes extend to nondiscriminatory burdens, they effectively authorize statutory religious exemptions, but they do so generally, not specifically. Thus, courts are required to apply the statutory strict scrutiny and to grant relief—typically in the form of religion-based exemptions—whenever they find that substantial burdens cannot be justified. Although hardly a substitute for constitutional Free Exercise protection, these broadly written statutes suggest that "leaving accommodation to the political process" need not disadvantage minority religions. Because they proceed generally, moreover, these statutes also overcome the problem of legislative anticipation; that is, they do not require speculative legislative judgments about the potential application of particular statutes to religious conduct.

In the previous chapter, we noted that these recent statutes, especially the ones adopted by Congress, raise significant constitutional questions entirely apart from the Establishment Clause. Putting those questions aside, however, the statutes appear to qualify as permissible accommodation. Justice Stevens once argued otherwise, contending that RFRA—and by implication any comparable statute—violates the Establishment Clause by favoring religious exercise over nonreligious conduct.[46] But this argument appears to ignore the Supreme Court's permissible accommodation doctrine. Not only do the statutes satisfy the two primary requirements we have identified, they do so by their express terms. Thus, RFRA, RLUIPA, and their state-law analogues are explicitly designed to redress substantial burdens on the exercise of religion, and they are broadly nonsectarian, extending to religious exercise of all sorts. To be sure, there might be a problem of sectarian discrimination if the Supreme Court were to define the exercise of religion broadly for constitutional purposes and if the statutes, by contrast, were confined to practices that were conventionally religious. Under this scenario, the statutes indeed would violate the Establishment Clause because they would prefer some "religions" over others. This constitutional problem could readily be avoided, however, by interpreting

46. *See* City of Boerne v. Flores, 521 U.S. 507, 536–37 (1997) (Stevens, J., concurring).

the statutes to follow the constitutional definition, so that the statutes themselves would extend to all religious exercise within the meaning of the Constitution, whether that exercise was conventionally religious or not.

In its 2005 decision in *Cutter v. Wilkinson*,[47] the Supreme Court (including Justice Stevens, who silently joined the opinion) unanimously rejected an Establishment Clause challenge to that portion of RLUIPA that authorizes religious exemption claims by institutionalized persons, typically prisoners. The Court noted that because of their confinement, institutionalized persons can face not only substantial but "exceptional" governmentally imposed burdens on their religious exercise, clearly justifying permissible accommodation. It also emphasized that the protection of RLUIPA extends to any and all religions, without sectarian discrimination, and it implied that the statute could and should be construed to avoid any Establishment Clause issues that might arise in particular applications. Although some of the Court's reasoning was specific to the institutionalized-persons context, *Cutter* strongly suggests that the Establishment Clause likewise does not invalidate the remainder of RLUIPA, nor RFRA or its state-law counterparts.[48]

As we have discussed, the doctrine of permissible accommodation is informed by Free Exercise con-

47.   544 U.S. 709 (2005).

48.   *Cf.* Gonzales v. O Centro Espirita Beneficente Uniao do Vegetal, 546 U.S. 418 (2006) (applying RFRA without questioning its validity under the Establishment Clause).

siderations. Because the Free Exercise Clause is directed to governmental action, it has no application to private burdens on the exercise of religion. Even so, there may be some room for the government to promote religious freedom by providing religion-based exemptions even from privately imposed burdens. For example, it appears that the Establishment Clause is not offended by a provision in Title VII of the Civil Rights Act of 1964 that requires (secular) employers, including private employers, to "reasonably accommodate" the religious practices of their employees if they can do so without "undue hardship." Conversely, in its 1985 decision in *Estate of Thornton v. Caldor, Inc.*,[49] the Supreme Court invalidated a state law that barred private employers from requiring employees to work on their Sabbath. Unlike the Title VII provision, the Sabbath law was categorical, not flexible; it took no account of the competing interests of employers or other employees.[50] It also singled out a particular religious practice for special protection, raising concerns of sectarian favoritism. Invoking the endorsement test to explain the distinction, Justice O'Connor suggested that an objective observer would view the Sabbath law as an endorsement of a particular religious belief, but would see

49. 472 U.S. 703 (1985).

50. In other cases, the Supreme Court has suggested, without clear elaboration, that the consideration of competing interests is relevant even in the context of governmentally imposed burdens. In *Cutter*, for example, the Court, relying on *Caldor*, stated that there is a general Establishment Clause requirement that "an accommodation must be measured so that it does not override other significant interests." *Cutter*, 544 U.S. at 722.

the more flexible and general Title VII provision, within the context of Title VII generally, as a legitimate means for protecting religious employees from improper and unjustified employment discrimination.[51]

The Dominant Position of the Lemon and Endorsement Tests in the Supreme Court's General Establishment Clause Doctrine

Accommodation is important both as a general concept and as a specialized field of Establishment Clause inquiry. It is doctrinally exceptional in a fundamental sense, however, because accommodation is permitted on the ground that it provides no benefit to religion that is constitutionally cognizable under the Establishment Clause. Outside the context of accommodation, virtually any assistance to religion can be seen as a cognizable benefit, and the critical question is whether the benefit is impermissible. In answering this question, the Supreme Court employs the three general tests discussed earlier in this section—Lemon, endorsement, and coercion—supplemented by an implicit exception for traditional governmental practices. The exception based on tradition is narrow. It appears to extend only to selected governmental practices that favor religion in a manner that is traditional, nonsectarian, and symbolic rather than tangible or coercive. The coercion test likewise has limited doctrinal importance. It plays a role in confining the tradition exception, but it is largely superfluous in the broad-

51. See Caldor, 472 U.S. at 711–12 (O'Connor, J., concurring).

er run of Establishment Clause cases. There, the *Lemon* and endorsement tests govern. Because those tests are more restrictive than the coercion test, the coercion test does little more than identify an especially troublesome subset of constitutional violations.

In most Establishment Clause cases, then, the critical inquiry is whether governmental benefits to religion are impermissible, and the controlling general doctrine—despite persistent criticism—is that of the *Lemon* and endorsement tests. These tests are not identical, but their elements overlap substantially. Indeed, the two tests can be combined into a single, more unitary inquiry. Under this analysis, governmental action runs afoul of the Establishment Clause if it violates any of three constitutional prohibitions. First, the government cannot act with the purpose of advancing or endorsing religion (either one religion or religion generally); instead, it must have a secular purpose for its action. Whether phrased in terms of advancement or endorsement, this first prohibition protects the value of formal religious equality by preventing the government from purposefully discriminating in favor of religion (either one religion or religion generally) through the award of deliberately discriminatory benefits. Second, even if the government has a secular purpose, its action cannot have the primary effect of advancing or endorsing religion (either one religion or religion generally). As discussed earlier, this second prohibition takes on a somewhat different meaning—less quantitative and concrete, more qualitative and symbolic—when it is phrased in terms of endorsement rather than advancement. Under either phrasing, however, the second prohibition can reach benefits to religion that are not deliberately discriminatory. As a result, this prohibition goes beyond formal equality and serves other constitutional values. Third, the governmental action cannot create an excessive governmental entanglement with religion. This third prohibition, which now is sometimes viewed as part of the second, addresses institutional separation and suggests a concern for structural constitutional values.

The Supreme Court's Establishment Clause doctrine is dominated by the *Lemon* and endorsement tests, with coercion, tradition, and accommodation playing subsidiary roles. Taken as a whole, these tests and considerations provide useful doctrinal guidelines. To more fully understand the Supreme Court's Establishment Clause doctrine, however, we need to know how the Court has elaborated and applied its general standards. We have already examined the concept of accommodation at this more particular level. In the remainder of this chapter, we will explore the Court's decisionmaking in several other areas of Establishment Clause concern: religion and the public schools; religious symbolism in other public contexts; and public aid to religious schools, organizations, and individuals.

Religion and the Public Schools

Prayer and Religious Instruction

In a long line of cases dating from 1948 to the present, the Supreme Court has invalidated school-sponsored prayer and religious instruction in the public schools, even when student participation is designated as voluntary. Apart from the aberrational case of *Zorach v. Clauson*,[52] the Court has consistently reasoned that the public schools cannot purposefully favor either specific religions or religion in general. The Court's decisions, including those decided before the *Lemon* and endorsement tests were formulated, rest on what is now the first prong of those tests. This prong forbids the government, including the public schools, from acting with the purpose of advancing or endorsing either one religion over others or religion over irreligion. Any such purposeful advancement or endorsement confers benefits on religion that are deliberately discriminatory and therefore impermissible. Since the government is not acting to remove a substantial burden on the exercise of religion, arguments of accommodation are unavailing. Arguments based on tradition are likewise unpersuasive. Even if a public-school practice promotes prayer or religious instruction in a manner that is both traditional and nonsectarian, and even if participation is formally voluntary, the risk of coercion in the public school context is sufficient to rule out the implicit exception.[53]

52. 343 U.S. 306 (1952).

53. *But cf. supra* notes 27–30 and accompanying text (suggesting that the implicit exception might permit school-spon-

The Court's decisionmaking in this context reflects the constitutional value of religious equality, which includes equality not only between and among religions, but also between religion and irreligion. Because the Court's decisions are directed to purposeful governmental discrimination, they can be fully explained in terms of formal equality. Even so, formal religious equality in this context also tends to promote substantive religious equality—not only for students, but also for parents, who have an interest in inculcating the religious or irreligious values of their choice. For simplicity, the discussion that follows will speak only of students, but the analysis clearly implicates the interests of parents as well.

The actions that are constitutionally forbidden—school-sponsored prayer and religious instruction—are actions that would impair substantive religious equality by their unequal impact on students of differing religions or of no religion at all. The impact on dissenting students could be considerable, and it could significantly impair other constitutional values. Certainly, the religious identity of the dissenting students would be threatened, and they would be likely to feel exclusion, affront, and alienation. Given the requirement of compulsory attendance and the impressionability of children, moreover, there also would be a substantial risk to religious voluntarism. In other words, the schools'

sored recitations of the Pledge of Allegiance, complete with its "under God" language, as long as students are not directly or substantially coerced to actively join the recitations).

promotion of religion might have its intended effect, inducing children to adopt religious beliefs and practices that they otherwise would not. At the very least, there would be "subtle coercive pressure" of the sort identified in *Lee v. Weisman*, as discussed earlier. The Court's doctrine in this area may also serve structural constitutional values, promoting a religiously inclusive political community even as it allows religion to thrive and compete in the private domain, free from the potentially debasing and corrosive effects of governmental involvement.

The Supreme Court's initial encounter with religion and the public schools was in 1948, only a year after *Everson v. Board of Education*.[54] In *Everson*, the Court had declared that the Establishment Clause forbids the government from aiding either one religion or religion in general. In *Illinois ex rel. McCollum v. Board of Education*,[55] the Court relied on this principle to invalidate a public school program that provided religious instruction through a "released-time" arrangement. Under the program, weekly classes in religious instruction, taught by privately employed religious teachers representing various faiths, were conducted in the school building during regular school hours. The classes were offered only to students whose parents had requested that they attend; students not attending continued their secular studies. The Court noted the challengers' argument that the program was voluntary in name only, and it also noted the fact of

54. 330 U.S. 1 (1947).
55. 333 U.S. 203 (1948).

compulsory school attendance. But the Court did not base its decision on coercion. Instead, the Court ruled that the program of religious instruction was unconstitutional because it singled out religion for special, advantageous treatment. By adopting and implementing this program, the public school had purposefully promoted religion over irreligion in violation of what would later become the first prong of the *Lemon* and endorsement tests.

Four years later, by contrast, the Court in *Zorach v. Clauson*[56] upheld a very similar program of religious released-time. In *Zorach*, as in *McCollum*, the challenged program offered weekly religious instruction by privately employed religious teachers of various faiths, with the classes taught during regular school hours to students whose parents requested that they attend, and with nonparticipating students continuing their secular studies. Unlike in *McCollum*, however, the religious classes in *Zorach* were conducted off the premises of the public schools, at religious centers to which the participating students retreated. For the Court in *Zorach*, this made all the difference, because now the public schools were doing "no more than accommodat[ing] their schedules to a program of outside religious instruction."[57] The Court's attempt to distinguish *McCollum* was tenuous. Yes, the on-the-premises program in *McCollum* may have favored religion to a greater degree than the off-the-premises program in *Zorach*. Both before and after *Zorach*, however,

56. 343 U.S. 306 (1952).

57. *Id.* at 315.

the Court has consistently ruled that the public schools cannot to *any* degree promote religion over irreligion by purposefully favoring the former over the latter. Yet purposeful favoritism is precisely what happens in a religious released-time program, regardless of where the religious instruction takes place. The public schools give special treatment to religion, and to religion alone, in an attempt to facilitate and promote religious instruction. This preferential treatment confers a discriminatory benefit on religion, and it violates what is now the first prong of the *Lemon* and endorsement tests.

In defending its decision in *Zorach*, the Court invoked the concept of accommodation, but the accommodation argument is weak. As the Court's more recent decisions have clarified, the concept of accommodation permits religion-based governmental action only if it is designed to provide relief from what would otherwise be a substantial burden on the exercise of religion—a direct or indirect burden that dissuades or discourages the exercise of religion by exerting substantial coercive pressure on religious decisionmaking. In the circumstances presented by *Zorach*, it is difficult to find such a burden. Compulsory attendance at a public school, where students must focus on secular subjects, restricts the time available for religious instruction, but students remain free to pursue such instruction during the many hours when school is not in session. As a result, it is difficult to argue that the public schools are either prohibiting religious conduct or placing religious students on the horns of a dilemma in their religious decisionmaking. Religious released-time programs, whether of the *Zorach* or of the *McCollum* variety, seem designed less to remove a burden on religious exercise than to confer an affirmative benefit on religion. As such, they are not strong candidates for an accommodation analysis.

Tenuous at the time the case was decided, the reasoning of *Zorach* is even more dubious today. Despite numerous decisions undermining its premises, however, *Zorach* has not been overruled, and off-the-premises released-time programs remain valid as a matter of prevailing constitutional law. Thus, *Zorach* stands—but as a decidedly aberrational decision.

In the years since *Zorach*, the Supreme Court has decided a number of Establishment Clause challenges to school-sponsored prayer and devotional exercises in the public schools. Unlike in *Zorach*, the Court in these cases has consistently honored what is now the first prong of the *Lemon* and endorsement tests. Accordingly, the Court has repeatedly invalidated laws and policies promoting school-sponsored prayer or devotion, even if nonsectarian and formally voluntary, on the ground that the government, including the public schools, cannot purposefully advance or endorse religion over irreligion.

The Supreme Court first addressed the classic form of school-sponsored prayer and devotion: spoken exercises in the classroom. In 1962, in *Engel v.*

Vitale,[58] the Court struck down a program that called for teachers to lead their students in a daily, state-prescribed prayer. The prayer was brief and nondenominational, and objecting students were permitted to opt out, but these factors did not save the program from invalidation. A year later, in *School District of Abington Township v. Schempp*,[59] the Court extended *Engel* to public school policies that did not involve a state-prescribed prayer, but that instead required a reading of Bible verses to non-objecting students and their collective recitation of the Lord's Prayer. Although the Court's opinion in *Schempp* foreshadowed what later became the first and second prongs of the *Lemon* test, its decision in this case, as in *Engel*, rested easily on the first prong alone. Whether or not the state actually composes a prayer or devotional reading, to call for its recitation in the classroom is undeniably an action that purposefully advances religion over irreligion, conferring a discriminatory benefit that is constitutionally impermissible.

Justice Stewart, the sole dissenter in *Engel* and *Schempp*, suggested that school-sponsored religious exercises generally should be upheld in the absence of demonstrable coercion. In his dissenting opinion in *Schempp*, he advanced an accommodation argument, contending that the challenged school policies furthered Free Exercise values. As in *Zorach* and for similar reasons, however, it is difficult to see the challenged policies in either *Engel* or *Schempp* as

58. 370 U.S. 421 (1962).

59. 374 U.S. 203 (1963).

attempts to remove what would otherwise be governmentally imposed, substantial burdens on the exercise of religion. In the absence of these policies, the public schools would not be promoting religion during the school day, but, given the limited hours of compulsory attendance, neither would the schools be prohibiting religious students from engaging in religious conduct nor placing them on the horns of a dilemma in their religious decisionmaking. It seems clear that the challenged policies of school-sponsored prayer and devotion were designed to advance religion, not religious freedom.

Some two decades later, in its 1985 decision in *Wallace v. Jaffree*,[60] the Supreme Court ruled that even policies that call for moments of silence in public school classrooms can violate the Establishment Clause, but only if the policies are purposefully crafted to promote the use of these moments for silent *prayer*. In *Wallace*, the Court addressed a 1981 Alabama statute that authorized a period of classroom silence "for meditation or voluntary prayer." Significantly, pre-existing Alabama law had already authorized a period of silence "for meditation," and the stark legislative history of the 1981 enactment confirmed that it was "entirely motivated by a purpose to advance religion" by "convey[ing] a message of State endorsement and promotion of prayer."[61] Accordingly, the Court concluded that the 1981 legislative action was unconstitutional under the first prong of the *Lemon* and

60.   472 U.S. 38 (1985).

61.   *Id.* at 56, 59.

endorsement tests. Conversely, the Court's opinion suggested that a moment-of-silence law not mentioning prayer would be constitutionally permissible. Taking into account the views of the five justices who wrote concurring and dissenting opinions, moreover, it appears that the Court likewise would have approved a law that did mention prayer as one permissible use for a moment of silence—as long as the law's language and history did not reveal the impermissible purpose of favoring and endorsing silent prayer over other forms of quiet reflection.

In more recent cases, the Supreme Court has invalidated school-sponsored prayer outside the classroom setting. As discussed earlier in this chapter, the Court in *Lee v. Weisman*[62] held that it was unconstitutional for a public school to sponsor a clergy-led, nonsectarian prayer at a graduation ceremony. And in *Santa Fe Independent School District v. Doe*,[63] the Court invalidated a school board policy that called for student votes to determine whether there would be student-led "invocation[s] and/or message[s]" before high school football games, in part "to solemnize" the games. A six-justice majority found that the policy violated the Establishment Clause, largely because its transparent purpose, as revealed by the policy's text and context, was to preserve and promote the school district's long-standing practice of school-sanctioned prayers at the games. As in its 1992 opinion in *Weisman*, the Court's 2000 opinion in *Doe* found indirect and

62.   505 U.S. 577 (1992).
63.   530 U.S. 290 (2000).

subtle coercion even in the absence of compulsory attendance. By the time of *Doe*, however, the Court had resumed its explicit reliance on the *Lemon* and endorsement tests. Under those tests and under the reasoning of the Court's other school prayer decisions, public school practices and policies of the sort confronted in *Weisman* and *Doe* are clearly invalid. In each case, there is governmental action that purposefully advances and endorses religion over irreligion, and that is enough to render it unconstitutional.[64]

It is important to emphasize that prayer and religious instruction are not themselves unconstitutional, even if they occur on the premises of public schools. What is unconstitutional is governmental sponsorship or promotion of these activities, either by law or through the policies or practices of public school boards, officials, or teachers. The government, including the public schools, cannot purposefully advance or endorse religion over irreligion. Students and other private actors, by contrast, are perfectly free to advance or endorse religion themselves, even in the context of the public schools. Indeed, they are constitutionally protected in this activity, primarily on the basis of free speech principles, as discussed in Chapter 5.

Freedom of speech, first and foremost, means that students can engage in personal prayer and

64. For the same reason, it is unconstitutional for the public schools to promote religion by posting the Ten Commandments in their buildings. *See* Stone v. Graham, 449 U.S. 39 (1980) (summarily invalidating a state law that required public schools to post the Ten Commandments in their classrooms).

other religious expression, even during the school day, subject only to the same regulations that apply to other sorts of student speech. Public schools cannot target the personal religious expression of students for special disadvantage, and even content-neutral regulations must be constitutionally reasonable. Students certainly are free, for example, to engage in silent prayer during a quiet time in class or nondisruptive spoken prayer in the hallway or the lunchroom. (As the saying goes, as long as there are math tests, there will be prayer in the public schools!)

According to the Supreme Court's "equal access" doctrine, moreover, freedom of speech gives private religious groups the right to use public school buildings, after hours, on the same basis as other private groups. This doctrine applies to noncurricular student groups,[65] and it also applies to community groups. In its 1993 decision in *Lamb's Chapel v.*

65. In *Widmar v. Vincent*, 454 U.S. 263 (1981), the Supreme Court ruled that state universities were required to give equal access to student groups that wished to use university facilities for religious worship and religious discussion. Congress then extended the policy of *Widmar* to public secondary schools by statute, through the Equal Access Act of 1984, and the Supreme Court later upheld the Act against an Establishment Clause challenge. *See* Board of Educ. of Westside Community Schools v. Mergens, 496 U.S. 226 (1990). In *Good News Club v. Milford Central School*, 533 U.S. 98 (2001), which is further discussed in the next paragraph of the text, the Court ruled that freedom of speech demands that the requirement of equal access be extended to public elementary schools as well. At least after *Good News Club*, it seems that the Equal Access Act does little or nothing more than the First Amendment itself requires as a matter of freedom of speech.

Center Moriches Union Free School District,[66] for example, the Court ruled that a public school district, having opened its facilities for after-hours use by a variety of community groups, could not exclude a religious group that wanted to present a film series promoting "Christian family values."

More recently, in a 2001 decision, the Court extended the equal access doctrine even to after-school religious meetings for elementary students. In *Good News Club v. Milford Central School*,[67] a Christian organization requested permission to conduct meetings for elementary school students immediately after school, meetings at which the children would sing songs, hear Bible lessons, memorize scripture, and pray. School policy permitted privately sponsored after-school meetings for various purposes, including morals and character education for children, but it prohibited the use of school facilities "for religious purposes." Citing this prohibition as well as the Establishment Clause, the school denied the organization's request. The Supreme Court ruled that the school's policy, as applied to the proposed meetings, amounted to impermissible viewpoint discrimination and therefore violated freedom of speech. Contrary to the school's argument, moreover, the Court found that the policy was not redeemed by the Establishment Clause. The Court reasoned that although the Clause forbids public schools from advancing or endorsing religion, this does not occur when schools merely

66. 508 U.S. 384 (1993).

67. 533 U.S. 98 (2001).

provide the sort of nondiscriminatory access that the Christian organization was seeking—possible misperceptions to the contrary notwithstanding. (Later in the chapter, we will more fully address the Establishment Clause analysis of public aid to religious organizations, including aid in the form of equal access to governmental property or other nondiscriminatory benefits.)

Evolution and Creationism

At least since the notorious *Scopes* case of the 1920s,[68] there has been tremendous controversy concerning the topic of human origins and how it should be taught in the public schools. The Supreme Court has declared that the Establishment Clause imposes significant limitations in this context. In essence, the Court has treated creationism as a matter of religious instruction, bringing into play the same sort of reasoning that the Court has applied to school-sponsored prayer and religious instruction generally. Thus, in its 1968 decision in *Epperson v. Arkansas*[69] and its 1987 decision in *Edwards v. Aguillard*,[70] the Court invalidated laws that were designed to prohibit the teaching of evolution or to promote the teaching of creationism. The Court found that the challenged laws were intended to protect and further a religious understanding of human origins. As such, they had the purpose of advancing and endorsing religion over irreligion, thereby conferring benefits on religion

68. *See* Scopes v. State, 289 S.W. 363 (Tenn. 1927).

69. 393 U.S. 97 (1968).

70. 482 U.S. 578 (1987).

that were deliberately discriminatory and constitutionally impermissible.

In *Epperson*, the Court invalidated an Arkansas law that had been enacted in 1928, in the aftermath of the *Scopes* case. Like the Tennessee law at issue in *Scopes*, the Arkansas law prohibited public school teachers from teaching "the theory or doctrine that mankind ascended or descended from a lower order of animals." Focusing on the history of the law, the Court concluded that "fundamentalist sectarian conviction was and is the law's reason for existence" and that the law prohibited the teaching of human evolution "for the sole reason that it is deemed to conflict with a particular religious doctrine; that is, with a particular interpretation of the Book of Genesis by a particular religious group."[71] As a result, the law violated what is now the first prong of the *Lemon* test. It had the purpose of advancing religion, and, indeed, a particular religion, in this case by protecting the religion from competing views. Relying on other grounds, Justice Black concurred in the Court's result, but he questioned the religious neutrality of the Court's reasoning, noting that the teaching of evolution could "infringe[ ] the religious freedom of those who consider evolution an anti-religious doctrine."[72]

Going a step beyond its ruling in *Epperson*, the Court in *Edwards* invalidated a Louisiana "balanced treatment" statute. The Louisiana statute did not preclude the teaching of evolution, at least

71. *Epperson*, 393 U.S. at 103, 108.

72. *Id.* at 113 (Black, J., concurring in the result).

not categorically; rather, it declared that any public school that elected to teach evolution was required to teach "creation science" as well. The state claimed that creation science reflected legitimate scientific opinion that had been improperly repressed, and it contended that the statute permitted students to confront the competing evidence and decide the matter for themselves. Over a vigorous dissent by Justice Scalia, however, the Court rejected the state's arguments and concluded that its secular defense of the statute was a "sham." The Court noted that public school teachers are free to teach genuinely scientific evidence about human origins, even if this evidence might undermine or place in question the prevailing theory of evolution, and it suggested that a legislature would be free to require that the public schools include this type of scientific critique. Based on the content of the Louisiana statute and its legislative history, however, the Court found that it was not designed to promote the teaching of diverse scientific theories. Rather, the legislature's "primary" and "preeminent" purpose was to advance and endorse a particular religious understanding of creation, an understanding that appeared to be drawn from a literal reading of Genesis. Accordingly, this statute, like the one in *Epperson*, violated the first prong of the *Lemon* and endorsement tests.[73]

73. *See Edwards*, 482 U.S. at 585–95; *see also id.* at 597–604 (Powell, J., concurring). The Supreme Court has not addressed the concept of "intelligent design," but, in a prominent ruling, a district court has concluded that it, too, should be treated as a religious understanding of creation that cannot be advanced or

Justice Black's separate opinion in *Epperson*, invoking the religious freedom of those who reject evolution, raises the possibility of a Free Exercise objection to the study of evolution in the public schools, at least as a required subject. Although our focus here is on the Establishment Clause, the Free Exercise issue deserves comment. Under contemporary Free Exercise doctrine, as discussed in Chapter 5, a claim for constitutional relief from the compulsory study of evolution might be viable, but it would be difficult to maintain. In the first place, the challenger would have to show that studying evolution would impose a substantial burden on the exercise of religion by exerting substantial coercive pressure on the student's religious understanding of creation. Even if the challenger could make this showing, that alone would not be enough to trigger heightened scrutiny under the Free Exercise doctrine of *Employment Division v. Smith*,[74] because the burden would be nondiscriminatory, a product of the school's general curriculum. One possible route around *Smith* would be a hybrid-claim argument, citing the right of parents to control the education of their children and attempting to rely upon and extend *Wisconsin v. Yoder*,[75] which the Court in *Smith* claimed not to disturb. If this argument succeeded, the challenger would achieve heightened constitutional scrutiny, but that still

endorsed by public schools. *See* Kitzmiller v. Dover Area Sch. Dist., 400 F. Supp. 2d 707 (M.D. Pa. 2005).

74. 494 U.S. 872 (1990).

75. 406 U.S. 205 (1972).

would not guarantee a religious exemption from the curricular requirement. The remaining question would be whether the compulsory study of evolution, as an important aspect of contemporary science, could survive the heightened scrutiny.[76]

Teaching About Religion

Under the Supreme Court's Establishment Clause cases, public schools are forbidden from promoting religion through school-sponsored prayer or religious instruction, including instruction that advances a religious understanding of creation. There is a critical distinction, however, between the public schools' promotional teaching *of* religion, which is constitutionally forbidden, and their objective teaching *about* religion, which is not. The public schools cannot purposefully advance or endorse religion (either one religion or religion generally) by promoting a religious perspective as true or sound. Conversely, schools are free to present and describe religion, including competing religious understandings, as part of a secular program of education.

The Supreme Court first embraced this distinction in its 1963 decision in *School District of Abington Township v. Schempp*.[77] The Court in *Schempp* invalidated public school policies that called for the devotional reading of Bible verses and the recitation of the Lord's Prayer, but it emphasized that its

76. For a pre-*Smith* lower court decision addressing and rejecting a Free Exercise claim analogous to that described in this paragraph, see Mozert v. Hawkins County Bd. of Educ., 827 F.2d 1058 (6th Cir. 1987).

77. 374 U.S. 203 (1963).

ruling did not extend to the "study of the Bible or of religion, when presented objectively as part of a secular program of education." The Court stated that "the Bible is worthy of study for its literary and historic qualities" and that public school students might appropriately study other religious subjects as well, including comparative religion, the history of religion, and the relationship of religion to the advancement of civilization.[78] In later cases, the Court has preserved and reaffirmed the distinction introduced in *Schempp*, suggesting, for example, that public schools can discuss the Ten Commandments "in an appropriate study of history, civilization, ethics, comparative religion, or the like."[79] Following the same reasoning, public schools likewise would be free to discuss and explain religious understandings of creation, assuming that the schools maintained their required objectivity.

Needless to say, there is a fine line between the neutral and objective teaching *about* religion and the partisan or promotional teaching *of* religion. The question necessarily turns on the specific content and context of the teaching, including the age of the students. Some public schools and public school teachers might be inclined to test the limits of permissible teaching, or they might deliberately cross the line from objectivity to religious partisanship. Conversely, other schools and teachers might steer away from any mention of religion, perhaps

78. *Id.* at 225.

79. Stone v. Graham, 449 U.S. 39, 42 (1980).

wishing to avoid any risk of Establishment Clause challenges or perhaps wishing simply to avoid controversy. As the Supreme Court itself suggested in *Schempp*, however, one's education is not complete without an understanding of religion and its historical and contemporary significance. Despite the difficulties, it seems that teaching about religion is sound educational policy. In any event, such teaching is constitutionally permissible.

Religious Symbolism Outside the Public School Context

The Supreme Court has decided a large number of Establishment Clause cases alleging impermissible benefits to religion outside the public school context. Many of them involve the inclusion of religious beneficiaries (including private religious schools or their students or parents) in public programs of financial aid or other tangible support. We will consider those cases in the next section. In this section, by contrast, the alleged benefits to religion are primarily and fundamentally symbolic. The challenged governmental actions provide no significant tangible support to religion and likewise present no serious claim of coercion. Examples include the use of religious symbols in public displays, such as Christmas displays, as well as references to God or religion in official declarations, such as our national motto.

As in its public school cases, the Supreme Court generally has addressed these religious symbolism cases by using the *Lemon* and endorsement tests. In this context as in that one, the government is not acting to remove a substantial burden on the exercise of religion, and arguments of accommodation are therefore unavailing. Unlike in the public school context, however, there is little or no risk of meaningful coercion here, not even indirect and subtle coercion of the sort discussed in *Lee v. Weisman*.[80] Accordingly, if the challenged religious symbolism is highly traditional, as well as nonsectarian, it may fall within the Court's implicit, tradition-based exception to the *Lemon* and endorsement tests. This implicit exception honors the value of tradition, which serves as a counterweight to other constitutional values. Thus, as discussed earlier, the Court relied heavily on tradition in its decision upholding the constitutionality of legislative prayer.[81] Likewise, it has implied that it would uphold other traditional governmental practices that are nonsectarian and essentially symbolic, even though they appear to advance and endorse religion in violation of the Court's usual Establishment Clause tests. As we emphasized in our earlier discussion, the contours of this implicit exception are quite uncertain, but permissible forms of religious symbolism might include presidential Thanksgiving proclamations; the Supreme Court's opening cry, "God Save the United States and this Honorable Court"; our na-

80. 505 U.S. 577 (1992).

81. Marsh v. Chambers, 463 U.S. 783 (1983).

tional motto, "In God We Trust"; and the "under God" language in the Pledge of Allegiance.

Whatever its precise contours, the tradition-based exception has a limited scope. Unless the government's action is supported by a deep and longstanding American tradition, even nonsectarian and purely symbolic governmental action is subject to the three-pronged analysis of the *Lemon* and endorsement tests. Accordingly, the Court has used this analysis to evaluate public displays, including holiday displays, that contain religious symbols. The Court has upheld some displays and rejected others.

The third prong of the analysis, concerning entanglement, has not been a major focal point in these cases. The first prong would seem highly relevant, but, unlike in the public school context, it has not always played a determinative role here. Instead, the Court sometimes has concluded, or else has assumed, that the government's purpose in including a religious symbol in a public display is not to advance or endorse religion, but instead is merely to "acknowledge" or "recognize" some aspect of religion that makes it relevant to the display. For example, a city might include a Christian nativity scene in a Christmas display to acknowledge or recognize the religious origins of Christmas. Under the first prong of the *Lemon* and endorsement tests, the government cannot act with the purpose of promoting religion, but it is free to address religion—in effect, to teach about religion, even outside the public school context—in a neutral and objective manner. Needless to say, the government's claim that it has included a religious symbol to serve this objective, non-promotional purpose may be highly contentious. In any event, a judicial evaluation of the government's purpose may be difficult, and it therefore is not surprising that the Court sometimes has passed over the first prong and focused its attention on the second.

Under the second prong of the *Lemon* and endorsement tests, governmental action, whatever its purpose, violates the Establishment Clause if it has the primary effect of advancing or endorsing religion. Because the context here is symbolic by nature, the Court has focused especially on the endorsement reformulation of the second prong, which, indeed, was first suggested by Justice O'Connor in a holiday display case, *Lynch v. Donnelly*.[82] Under this analysis, the question is whether a "reasonable observer" or an "objective observer," properly informed of the relevant history and context of the public display in question, would perceive a message of governmental endorsement of religion (either one religion or religion generally). This inquiry addresses the symbolic effect of the government's action, focusing on its objective or apparent meaning, not its intended purpose. Even so, if a reasonable, objective observer would conclude that the government is endorsing religion, it is likely that this is precisely the government's intention. Indeed, in its 2005 decision in *McCreary County v.*

82. 465 U.S. 668 (1984); *see id.* at 687–94 (O'Connor, J., concurring).

ACLU of Kentucky,[83] a Ten Commandments case to which we will return shortly, the Supreme Court largely equated the purpose and effect prongs in the context of religious symbolism, declaring that public displays should be found to rest on the impermissible purpose of advancing religion if a reasonable, objective observer would so conclude. With or without the explicit linkage invoked in *McCreary*, it seems that the second prong of the analysis is being used to police violations of the first, even as the Court avoids the treacherous evidentiary problems that a more direct evaluation of purpose would entail.

As *McCreary* makes clear, the Court's decision-making in this context can serve to prevent the purposeful endorsement of religion. But *McCreary*'s focus on the reasonable, objective observer, coupled with the Court's reliance upon the impermissible effect of endorsement in other cases, suggests that the inquiry here is not designed merely to preclude formal or deliberate discrimination. Instead, the governing analysis reflects a concern for the symbolic impact of the government's action, especially on dissenters, who may be affronted and alienated if the government appears to be endorsing religious beliefs they do not share. Thus, the Court's doctrine concerning religious symbolism promotes not merely formal religious equality, but also substantive equality. It gives special weight to the value of respecting the religious identity of dissenting citizens, and, relatedly, it serves the structural value of

83. 545 U.S. 844 (2005).

promoting a religiously inclusive political community.

The Court's analysis—whether under the endorsement variant of the second prong or under *McCreary*'s inquiry into objective purpose—requires sensitive judgments about the objective meaning of particular public displays, taking into account the particular history and setting of each display and the particular mix of symbols that it includes. In the Court's 1984 decision in *Lynch*, for instance, the Court upheld the use of a nativity scene in a municipal Christmas display that also included a Santa Claus house, reindeer, and other secular symbols. Although the majority opinion invoked and emphasized the original *Lemon* test, Justice O'Connor argued in her concurrence that the nativity scene, in context, did not have the effect of communicating a message of governmental endorsement of religion (either Christianity or religion in general). To O'Connor, the breadth of the city's overall display suggested a different and permissible governmental message—one that simply celebrated Christmas, a public and heavily secularized holiday, by giving recognition to its various traditional symbols. An objective observer, she concluded, would not believe that the government included the nativity scene to endorse its religious content.

Five years later, in *County of Allegheny v. ACLU*,[84] the Court itself adopted the endorsement reformulation of the second prong in its evaluation of two separate holiday displays. Shifting majorities

84.   492 U.S. 573 (1989).

held that a county-sponsored nativity scene was unconstitutional, but that it was permissible for a city to display a Chanukah menorah alongside a Christmas tree and a sign saluting liberty. Unlike the nativity scene in *Lynch*, this one was not part of a broader display that included secular symbols; it stood essentially alone in a prominent location within the county courthouse, and it included a banner proclaiming "Gloria in Excelsis Deo!" ("Glory to God in the Highest!"). Focusing on the objective meaning of the display, the Court found that in context, the nativity scene conveyed an impermissible message of governmental endorsement. Conversely, Justices Blackmun and O'Connor, casting the deciding votes concerning the menorah, concluded that its inclusion in the city's display conveyed a message that did not endorse Judaism or religion in general. Instead, when viewed with the other elements of the display, the menorah was part of an overall message that celebrated the secular dimensions of the winter holiday season (Justice Blackmun's position) or that promoted pluralism and freedom of belief (the view of Justice O'Connor).

In its 2005 decision in *McCreary* and in a companion case, *Van Orden v. Perry*,[85] the Supreme Court addressed public displays of the Ten Commandments. Four justices urged a new and more relaxed approach to "passive" religious symbolism outside the public school context,[86] but their view

85. 545 U.S. 677 (2005).

86. *See id.* at 686–92 (plurality opinion).

did not command a majority. Instead, a divided Supreme Court again offered a pair of mixed decisions, with the Court's competing results resting on the context-specific approach of *Lynch* and *Allegheny*, now linked to the inquiry into purpose. Thus, in *McCreary*, a five-justice majority invalidated recently erected courthouse displays of framed copies of the Ten Commandments. The Commandments were surrounded by the Magna Carta, the Declaration of Independence, the Bill of Rights, and other historical documents, but the current arrangements had been preceded by earlier, more limited displays that clearly were designed to promote the religious content of the Commandments. According to the Court, a reasonable, objective observer would conclude from the sequence of events that the current displays were intended to further the same, predominantly religious purpose as the displays they had replaced. In *Van Orden*, by contrast, a different five-justice majority upheld the constitutionality of a longstanding, forty-year-old display of the Ten Commandments on the outdoor grounds of the Texas State Capitol, where the Commandments stood as one monument among many in a large, park-like setting. Switching sides as he cast the deciding vote, Justice Breyer reasoned in his controlling opinion that unlike the displays in *McCreary*, the Texas monument, in its particular historical context and physical setting, conveyed a predominately secular message—a message about the Ten Commandments' historical significance and their importance to secular morality.[87]

The Supreme Court's context-specific approach extends to holiday and other public displays, including not only displays that are clearly sponsored by the government, but also private displays on governmental property. Needless to say, the private endorsement of religion is not unconstitutional, but if a private religious display is on governmental property, contextual considerations could suggest the improper appearance of governmental endorsement. If the property is a public forum open equally to religious and nonreligious displays, an Establishment Clause violation is highly unlikely. In its 1995 decision in *Capitol Square Review and Advisory Board v. Pinette*,[88] for example, the Supreme Court ruled that the Establishment Clause did not preclude a privately sponsored cross, accompanied by a sign disclaiming governmental sponsorship, from being accorded equal access to a traditional public forum. Even so, five justices, speaking through separate opinions, affirmed the need for a context-specific inquiry under the endorsement reformulation of the second prong.[89] In so doing, they specifi-

87. Justice Breyer claimed to rely on "legal judgment" in *Van Orden*, rather than *Lemon* or the endorsement test as such, but his "fact-intensive" analysis was largely consistent with the endorsement reformulation of the second prong, as well as *McCreary*'s inquiry into objective purpose. *See id.* at 698–706 (Breyer, J., concurring in the judgment).

88. 515 U.S. 753 (1995).

89. *See id.* at 772–83 (O'Connor, J., joined by Souter and Breyer, JJ., concurring in part and concurring in the judgment); *id.* at 783–96 (Souter, J., joined by O'Connor and Breyer, JJ., concurring in part and concurring in the judgment); *id.* at 797–

cally rejected the position of a four-justice plurality opinion, which argued that private religious speech can never be restricted in a public forum in order to avoid an Establishment Clause violation predicated on perceived governmental endorsement.[90]

Public Aid to Religious Schools, Organizations, and Individuals

We turn now to our final group of Establishment Clause cases. Like the religious symbolism cases, these cases involve claims of impermissible benefits to religion outside the public school context. Here, however, the benefits to religion are not primarily symbolic. Instead, they take the form of significant financial aid or other tangible support to religious beneficiaries, including religious schools, organizations, and individuals. Neither accommodation nor tradition is pertinent in this context. The governmental action does not qualify as accommodation because it is not designed to remove a substantial burden on the exercise of religion. Likewise, although some forms of tangible support might be traditional, the governmental action is not merely or essentially symbolic, and it therefore falls outside the tradition-based exception. No inquiry into coercion is required, and the coercion test therefore does not play a significant role in the analysis. With

816 (Stevens, J., dissenting); *id.* at 817–18 (Ginsburg, J., dissenting).

90. *See id.* at 763–70 (plurality opinion).

these other concepts and tests thus out of the picture, the Supreme Court's decisionmaking in this area has been governed by the basic Establishment Clause standards of the *Lemon* and endorsement tests.

Virtually without exception, the first requirement of constitutionality, that of secular purpose, has been readily satisfied in the public aid context. This requirement of formal equality forbids the government from acting with the purpose of advancing or endorsing religion (either one religion or religion generally) through the conferral of deliberately discriminatory benefits. But the challenged governmental actions in this area typically do not involve formal or deliberate discrimination. Rather, they are general programs of aid that include both religious and nonreligious beneficiaries, without distinction. As a result, the Court's decisions have hinged on the remaining portions of the analysis, addressing effect and entanglement.

The third prong of the analysis, precluding excessive entanglement between religion and government, sometimes has been an issue, especially when a program of aid requires close governmental supervision. In the bulk of the cases, however, the debate has centered on the second prong, which bars governmental action that has the primary effect of advancing or endorsing religion (either one religion or religion generally). Indeed, since 1997, the Court in the public aid context has formally weakened the doctrinal significance of entanglement by folding the third prong into the second and by treating entanglement as simply one aspect of the effect inquiry.[91]

In its 1971 opinion in *Lemon*, the Court declared that the second prong precludes programs of aid that have the "principal or primary effect" of advancing religion.[92] Supplemented to some degree by the endorsement reformulation, this general standard continues to be affirmed.[93] As stated, however, the standard is exceedingly vague, and it raises a variety of questions, including two that are basic. First, does the second prong preclude benefits to religion under a formally nondiscriminatory aid program if, in actual operation, the program has a discriminatory *effect* that favors religious beneficiaries? Second, does it preclude some benefits to religion even under programs that are *entirely* nondiscriminatory, not only formally but also in effect?

Depending on the answers to these basic questions and other, subsidiary ones, the Court's interpretation and enforcement of the Establishment Clause in this context might serve a variety of constitutional values, both individual and structural. Religious voluntarism might be threatened by benefit programs that induce individuals to modify their religious beliefs or practices in order to qualify. Relatedly, at a more structural level, the extension of benefits to religious beneficiaries, with conditions attached, might compromise the vitality of

91. *See* Agostini v. Felton, 521 U.S. 203, 232–33 (1997).

92. Lemon v. Kurtzman, 403 U.S. 602, 612 (1971).

93. *See, e.g.*, *Agostini*, 521 U.S. at 222–23, 235; Zelman v. Simmons–Harris, 536 U.S. 639, 648–49, 654–55 (2002).

religion and the autonomy of religious institutions. At the same time, an aid program that includes religious beneficiaries—even if the program is formally nondiscriminatory—might appear to endorse religion in a manner that disrespects the religious identity of dissenting citizens. Indeed, dissenting citizens might find it especially offensive that they are being forced to support, through their taxes, programs that have the effect of aiding religious beliefs and practices that are not their own. These feelings of offense and alienation in turn might undermine the religious inclusiveness of the political community.

Although all of these constitutional values are implicated in the public aid context, the value that has been the most influential, especially in recent cases, is that of religious equality. Understood in a strictly formal sense, this value would sanction any program of aid that is formally nondiscriminatory. Standing alone, therefore, it would suggest that the first prong of the analysis should be determinative, and that the second prong (and with it the remaining content of the third) should be jettisoned altogether. Understood in a more substantive sense, by contrast, the value of religious equality looks beyond the form or purpose of the governmental action. It honors religious equality, but with a focus on the actual impact of governmental action on religious and irreligious citizens and organizations. So understood, the value of religious equality would not sanction a formally nondiscriminatory program if, despite its form, it nonetheless had a discriminatory effect.

Everson v. Board of Education,[94] decided in 1947, was the Supreme Court's first modern case addressing the question of public aid. In *Everson*, the Court used strongly separationist language, but it nonetheless upheld a formally nondiscriminatory program of bus-fare reimbursement that extended to parents whose children were being transported to Roman Catholic schools. After *Everson*, the Court did not return to the public aid context for twenty years, but, since then, it has decided a large number of cases.

In the 1970s and 1980s, the Supreme Court approved some public aid programs, but it invalidated others. The Court's doctrine was muddled and depended on fine distinctions. Even so, it appeared to reflect a concern for religious equality in its substantive sense, as well as other constitutional values, both individual and structural. Indeed, in its invalidation of various programs, the Court sometimes appeared to adopt a strong and categorical interpretation of its separationist language in *Everson*, which had declared that the government cannot "pass laws which aid one religion [or] all religions" and that "[n]o tax in any amount, large or small, can be levied to support any religious activities or institutions, whatever they may be called, or whatever form they may adopt to teach or practice religion."[95] This interpretation suggested separationist responses to the two basic questions regarding the second prong of the *Lemon* test. First, it

94. 330 U.S. 1 (1947).

95. *Id.* at 15–16.

suggested that a formally nondiscriminatory aid program would be constitutionally problematic if it had a discriminatory effect that favored religion. Second, it implied—albeit more ambiguously—that public aid simply could not be extended to religious beneficiaries, not even if the program of aid was entirely nondiscriminatory, both in purpose and in effect.

More recently, by contrast, the Supreme Court's decisionmaking has shifted substantially, making its doctrine more coherent and simple, and at the same time far less separationist. The Court has emphasized formal equality more than substantive, and it has minimized the independent role of other constitutional values. The Court has suggested that formal equality itself tends to promote substantive equality and other constitutional values in this context, and that, in any event, increased doctrinal clarity is important. Indicating a retreat from more separationist responses to the two basic questions under the second prong, the Court has made it clear that formally nondiscriminatory programs of aid generally will be upheld—even if they extend to religious beneficiaries and even if they might appear, in practical effect, to discriminate in their favor. Nonetheless, the Court has not abandoned the second prong of the analysis altogether, and it continues to recognize some constitutional limits even on formally nondiscriminatory programs.

The Doctrinal Approach of the 1970s and 1980s

Beginning with *Lemon v. Kurtzman* itself[96] and continuing through a series of cases in the 1970s

96. Lemon v. Kurtzman, 403 U.S. 602 (1971). The Supreme Court decided one public aid case between *Everson* and *Lemon*.

and 1980s, the Supreme Court suggested that it would analyze public aid programs with an eye to various considerations, generally under the rubric of the second prong of the *Lemon* test. Almost all of these cases involved aid to religious schools or their students or parents. The Court's decisions rested on sometimes doubtful distinctions, and its decision-making criteria were decidedly ambiguous. Even so, at least five sorts of considerations appeared to be playing significant roles.

First, the Supreme Court addressed the manner in which the aid was provided. The Court was more likely to invalidate aid that was provided directly to the religious schools, and it was less likely to invalidate aid that was targeted initially to individual students or parents and that reached the religious schools only indirectly, as a result of individual choice. A program that directly reimbursed religious schools for educational expenses, for example, was more likely to be invalidated than a program of educational tax deductions that extended to parents who chose to educate their children at such schools.[97] As we will see later, this emphasis on the

In *Board of Education v. Allen*, 392 U.S. 236 (1968), the Court ruled that the Establishment Clause did not bar a state from lending secular textbooks, free of charge, to students at religious as well as other private and public schools.

97. *Compare Lemon*, 403 U.S. at 621 (invalidating a program of direct reimbursement, based in part on this constitutional

manner of aid—direct or indirect—has become a critical factor in contemporary doctrine. In the 1970s and 1980s, it was an important factor, but it did not appear to be as crucial as it plainly is today.

Second, the Court suggested that the quantity or percentage of aid reaching religious beneficiaries was a relevant consideration in evaluating the effect of a public aid program. Substantial benefits, or benefits that mainly assisted religious schools, were more likely to be invalidated.[98]

Third, the Court was more likely to invalidate programs of aid that were designed to benefit elementary or secondary education, as opposed to higher education. Although most religious colleges and universities have strong secular components, the Court described elementary and secondary religious schools as "pervasively sectarian"—religious through and through. At the same time, the younger age of the students made them more susceptible to the religious training and instruction that they received. For these reasons, the Court believed that public aid reaching religious beneficiaries in the context of elementary or secondary education was more likely to be used—and used successfully—to advance religion, suggesting a constitutionally impermissible effect. Conversely, the Court was more

"defect"), *with* Mueller v. Allen, 463 U.S. 388, 399 (1983) (approving a program of indirect funding through educational tax deductions and emphasizing, as one factor among others, that the aid did not involve "the direct transmission of assistance from the State to the schools themselves").

98. *See, e.g.*, Committee for Public Educ. & Religious Liberty v. Nyquist, 413 U.S. 756 (1973).

likely to uphold aid programs that were directed to higher education, even if religious colleges and universities were included.[99]

Fourth, the Court considered the substance of the aid being provided, with the question being whether this particular type of aid might itself be used to inculcate religion, again suggesting an improper effect. For example, providing instructional materials and equipment for use in religious schools was more problematic than providing textbooks on purely secular subjects, because the instructional materials and equipment could more readily be used for religious as well as secular education.[100] Aid that was clearly and effectively segregated to secular activities was more likely to be approved.

Fifth, the Court considered the extent to which a particular program of aid might require continuing governmental involvement and monitoring. Using what was then the separate third prong of the *Lemon* test, the Court reasoned that this kind of continuing relationship might create a constitutionally impermissible entanglement of religion and government.

99. *See* Tilton v. Richardson, 403 U.S. 672 (1971); Hunt v. McNair, 413 U.S. 734 (1973); Roemer v. Board of Public Works, 426 U.S. 736 (1976).

100. *Compare* Board of Educ. v. Allen, 392 U.S. 236 (1968) (approving aid in the form of secular textbooks), *with* Meek v. Pittenger, 421 U.S. 349 (1975), and Wolman v. Walter, 433 U.S. 229 (1977) (rejecting aid in the form of instructional materials and equipment). This specific distinction has since been expressly rejected, with *Meek* and *Wolman* being overruled on this point. *See* Mitchell v. Helms, 530 U.S. 793, 808, 835 (2000) (plurality opinion); *id.* at 837 (O'Connor, J., concurring in the judgment).

Two 1985 cases provide examples of the Supreme Court's reasoning in this period, and they also illustrate the Court's sometimes separationist decisionmaking. In *School District of Grand Rapids v. Ball*[101] and *Aguilar v. Felton*,[102] a deeply divided Court ruled that the Establishment Clause barred publicly paid teachers from providing secular, remedial education on the premises of primary and secondary religious schools. The challenged programs extended to religious and nonreligious schools alike, and the Court found that they had the purpose of supporting secular education, thereby satisfying the first prong of *Lemon*. Utilizing some of the considerations just outlined, however, the Court concluded that the programs could not survive the remainder of the analysis.

In *Grand Rapids*, the Supreme Court found that the challenged programs had the primary effect of advancing religion and therefore violated the second prong of *Lemon*. The Court stated that the programs impermissibly advanced the "sectarian enterprise" of the religious schools because the aid was "direct and substantial." Addressing the substance of the aid, the Court reasoned that the publicly funded teachers might knowingly or unwittingly "conform their instruction to the environment in which they teach," thereby furthering the schools' religious mission. In part as a result, the Court also concluded that the impressionable children attending the schools might perceive a "symbolic union of

101. 473 U.S. 373 (1985).

102. 473 U.S. 402 (1985).

church and state" reflecting an improper governmental endorsement of religion.[103] In *Aguilar*, the challenged program was designed to mitigate the Establishment Clause vices that the Court identified in *Grand Rapids*. In particular, it included a system of governmental monitoring to ensure that the remedial classes and therefore the aid would remain entirely secular, both in reality and in perception. That very system of monitoring, however, led the Court to find an excessive governmental entanglement with religion, this in violation of *Lemon*'s third prong.

Then–Justice Rehnquist's dissenting opinion in *Aguilar* lamented the "Catch–22" that he believed the Court had created.[104] His position has since prevailed, and *Grand Rapids* and *Aguilar* have been overruled.[105] Indeed, in hindsight, *Grand Rapids* and *Aguilar* represent the end of a doctrinal era. They are the last Supreme Court decisions to follow the complex and sometimes separationist approach of the 1970s and 1980s. Today, an approach along those lines is advanced only in dissenting opinions. It is worth noting, however, that these dissenting opinions are often joined by as many as four justices,[106] suggesting that this view still commands

103. *Grand Rapids*, 473 U.S. at 388, 390, 396.

104. *Aguilar*, 473 U.S. at 420–21 (Rehnquist, J., dissenting).

105. *See* Agostini v. Felton, 521 U.S. 203, 235–36 (1997) (overruling *Aguilar* in full and *Grand Rapids* in part).

106. *See, e.g., id.* at 240–54 (Souter, J., joined by Stevens and Ginsburg, JJ., and in part by Breyer, J., dissenting); Mitchell v. Helms, 530 U.S. 793, 867–913 (2000) (Souter, J., joined by Stevens and Ginsburg, JJ., dissenting); Zelman v. Simmons–

considerable support and that—with modest changes in the Court's membership—something like the approach of the 1970s and 1980s could conceivably return in the future.

Contemporary Doctrine Regarding Indirect Aid[107]

The contemporary Supreme Court has replaced the multifaceted approach of the 1970s and 1980s with a two-track doctrine for public aid cases, with the Court selecting one track or the other based upon the manner in which the aid is provided. Thus, the Court sharply distinguishes between direct aid, which flows directly from the government to religious schools or organizations, and indirect aid, which flows initially to individuals and which reaches religious schools or organizations only because the individual recipients, as a matter of private choice, elect to use it there.[108] As discussed earlier, the distinction between direct and indirect aid was a significant consideration under the doctrinal approach of the 1970s and 1980s. Over time, the

Harris, 536 U.S. 639, 686–717 (2002) (Souter, J., joined by Stevens, Ginsburg, and Breyer, JJ., dissenting); *id.* at 717–29 (Breyer, J., joined by Stevens and Souter, JJ., dissenting).

107. For a more elaborate discussion, including an analysis of Chief Justice Rehnquist's instrumental role in the development of this doctrine, see Daniel O. Conkle, *Indirect Funding and the Establishment Clause: Rehnquist's Triumphant Vision of Neutrality and Private Choice, in* The Rehnquist Legacy 54 (Craig M. Bradley ed., 2006).

108. The discussion that follows adheres to the stated distinction between direct and indirect aid. It is important to recognize, however, that there are other possible meanings of "direct" and "indirect" and that the Supreme Court itself sometimes uses these terms in a different or more general way.

importance of this distinction became increasingly apparent, but its overriding significance—in dividing cases into two separate doctrinal tracks–became clear only in 2002, when the Supreme Court decided *Zelman v. Simmons–Harris*.[109]

In *Zelman*, the Court rejected an Establishment Clause challenge to a school voucher program that provided substantial tuition support for low-income parents, who could use the support at religious as well as nonreligious schools. The program was formally nondiscriminatory, but over ninety percent of the vouchers were being used at religious schools. The program's purpose was concededly secular, and the Court concluded that the program likewise passed scrutiny under the effect prong. Of broader doctrinal consequence, the Court made it clear that indirect aid, as in *Zelman*, is subject to a different Establishment Clause analysis than direct aid. As we will see shortly, the Court's contemporary doctrine concerning direct aid is considerably more permissive than it was in the past, but direct aid remains subject to certain restrictions that apply even to formally nondiscriminatory programs. By contrast, the Court in *Zelman* suggested that a formally nondiscriminatory program of indirect aid is virtually immune from Establishment Clause invalidation, even if the final destination of the aid would suggest a strongly discriminatory effect.

Focusing on the second prong of the *Lemon* test and interpreting earlier cases to rest on similar reasoning, the Supreme Court declared in *Zelman*

109. 536 U.S. 639 (2002).

that "our decisions have drawn a consistent distinction between government programs that provide aid directly to religious schools and programs of true private choice, in which government aid reaches religious schools only as a result of the genuine and independent choices of private individuals."[110] As long as a program of indirect aid is formally nondiscriminatory and is "a program of true private choice" that is not "skewed" to create incentives favoring the selection of religious schools, the program "is not readily subject to challenge under the Establishment Clause."[111] Indeed, the Court emphasized that it had never invalidated such a program, and it implied that it never would. The Court suggested that programs of private choice honor the value of religious voluntarism, and that, in the absence of an improper "skewing" that favors or disfavors religious choices, formal equality in this context promotes substantive equality as well. The Court further argued that there is no improper appearance of *governmental* endorsement of religion even if individuals disproportionately direct their benefits to religious destinations. If not, then one might likewise conclude that these programs of private choice neither disrespect the religious identity of citizens nor undermine the religious inclusiveness of the political community.

With the benefit of hindsight, we can see the two-track approach—and the Supreme Court's consistent approval of formally nondiscriminatory pro-

110. *Id.* at 649 (citations omitted).

111. *Id.* at 649–53.

grams of indirect aid—in three earlier decisions that the Court cited and relied upon in *Zelman*. This series of cases stretches back to *Mueller v. Allen*,[112] which was decided in 1983, two years before *Grand Rapids* and *Aguilar* sounded the last hurrah for the doctrinal approach of the 1970s and 1980s. Given the multifaceted doctrine that prevailed at that time, the Court's reasoning in *Mueller* was more complex than the Court in *Zelman* was willing to admit. Even so, the Court in *Mueller* did rely heavily on the theme of private choice. In so doing, the Court approved a program of educational tax deductions for the parents of children attending religious as well as nonreligious schools, even though, as in *Zelman*, more than ninety percent of the aid in fact accrued to the benefit of individuals choosing religious schools.

In *Zelman*, the Supreme Court also cited its 1986 decision in *Witters v. Washington Department of Services for the Blind*[113] and its 1993 decision in *Zobrest v. Catalina Foothills School District*.[114] In *Witters*, the Court addressed a vocational scholarship program that provided tuition assistance to the visually impaired, and it ruled that the Establishment Clause did not forbid the extension of this aid to a blind student who had chosen to attend a religious college in preparation for a religious career. In like fashion, the Court in *Zobrest* ruled that a federal program providing sign-language inter-

112.   463 U.S. 388 (1983).

113.   474 U.S. 481 (1986).

114.   509 U.S. 1 (1993).

preters for deaf children could be extended to a student who was attending a religious high school.

Unlike in *Mueller*, the aid programs in *Witters* and *Zobrest* did not have the effect of disproportionately favoring religious institutions, not even indirectly, but the Court in *Zelman* made it clear that that feature of the programs was not essential to their constitutionality. "The constitutionality of a neutral educational aid program," the Court wrote, "simply does not turn on whether and why, in a particular area, at a particular time, most private schools are run by religious organizations, or most recipients choose to use the aid at a religious school."[115] More generally, when this track of the Court's doctrine is in play, the ultimate destination of the aid is beside the point, and there is no need whatever to segregate the aid to ultimate uses that are secular in nature. Likewise, the other factors that the Court invoked under the multifaceted doctrine of the 1970s and 1980s appear to be irrelevant. Thus, if the aid is provided indirectly, it does not matter whether it is substantial or whether it is designed to benefit elementary or secondary education, as opposed to higher education. It also appears that the indirect manner of funding is likely to defeat any claim of excessive governmental entanglement with religion.

In the wake of *Zelman*, formally nondiscriminatory programs of indirect aid are almost certain to be upheld. For example, *Zelman* strongly supports the constitutionality of federal and state "charitable

115. *Zelman*, 536 U.S. at 658.

choice" programs—recently promoted under the banner of a "faith-based initiative"—to the extent that they authorize social-service vouchers that recipients can use at the provider of their choice, whether or not the provider is a religious organization.

One question left unresolved by *Zelman* was whether the government even retains the constitutional *option* of excluding religious organizations from otherwise general programs of indirect, voucher-based funding for privately provided education or social services. Such an exclusion presumably would not violate the Establishment Clause, but would it violate the Free Exercise Clause? By excluding religious organizations and thereby precluding voucher recipients from choosing religious options, the government arguably would be imposing a substantial and discriminatory burden on religious decision-making, triggering strict scrutiny and probable invalidation. As discussed in Chapter 5, the Supreme Court's recent decision in *Locke v. Davey*[116] tends to undermine this Free Exercise argument, but the scope of the Court's decision is uncertain. *Locke* might be confined to the discriminatory denial of funding for the devotional religious work and training of clergy and other religious professionals. Conversely, and perhaps more likely, it might permit the government to exclude religious beneficiaries in other indirect funding contexts as well.[117] If so,

116.   540 U.S. 712 (2004).

117.   Lower courts have read *Locke* to permit the exclusion of religious schools from voucher programs for elementary and

then *Zelman* and *Locke*, taken together, would leave the inclusion or exclusion of religious beneficiaries largely to the discretion of Congress and the states.[118]

Contemporary Doctrine Regarding Direct Aid

What, then, of direct aid, that is, public aid that flows directly to religious schools or organizations? As *Zelman*'s two-track analysis suggests, direct aid is subject to Establishment Clause restrictions that do not apply to indirect aid. Indeed, under the doctrine of the 1970s and 1980s, the Supreme Court was generally inclined to invalidate direct aid, at least when the benefitted institutions were not merely religiously affiliated but "pervasively sectar-

secondary education. *See* Eulitt v. Maine, 386 F.3d 344 (1st Cir. 2004); Bush v. Holmes, 886 So.2d 340 (Fla. Dist. Ct. App. 2004) (en banc), *aff'd on other grounds*, 919 So.2d 392 (Fla. 2006). By contrast, in *Colorado Christian Univ. v. Weaver*, 534 F.3d 1245 (10th Cir. 2008), the court distinguished *Locke* in the course of invalidating a state-sponsored college scholarship program that excluded all students attending "pervasively sectarian" religious colleges.

118. Many state constitutions (including the Washington Constitution, as discussed in *Locke*) contain strongly worded prohibitions on public aid to religion. Some of these provisions, as a matter of state law, might require the exclusion of religious organizations even from programs of indirect aid. These state constitutional provisions would have to give way to the federal constitution if it were construed to demand a different result, but if *Locke* is read broadly, there may be no conflict. For a complete compilation of state constitutional prohibitions on aid to religion and an analysis of their significance, especially in the context of "charitable choice" programs, see Ira C. Lupu & Robert W. Tuttle, Government Partnerships with Faith–Based Service Providers: The State of the Law 35–41, 77–129 (The Roundtable on Religion and Social Welfare Policy, 2002).

ian"—a designation that the Court extended not only to churches, synagogues, and mosques, but also to primary and secondary religious schools. As in the context of indirect aid, however, the Supreme Court has moved away from its earlier doctrine, and the Court today is quite permissive even concerning direct aid. Contemporary doctrine is consistent with certain precedents from the 1970s and 1980s, but it is frankly inconsistent with others, and the Court has explicitly overruled a number of prior decisions. More generally, the Court now embraces a more lenient approach, one that emphasizes formal religious equality and that allows the Court to uphold most programs that are formally nondiscriminatory. Nonetheless, the Court's approach to direct aid is more complex than its approach to indirect aid, and formally nondiscriminatory programs remain subject to certain constitutional limitations.

The dominant features of the Supreme Court's contemporary doctrine concerning direct aid are marked by the Court's 1997 decision in *Agostini v. Felton*[119] and by its 2000 decision in *Mitchell v. Helms*.[120] In *Agostini*, the Supreme Court addressed the very same program of aid that it had considered twelve years earlier in *Aguilar v. Felton*.[121] Overruling *Aguilar* and the Court's companion ruling in *Grand Rapids v. Ball*,[122] the Court declared in

119.   521 U.S. 203 (1997).

120.   530 U.S. 793 (2000).

121.   473 U.S. 402 (1985).

122.   473 U.S. 373 (1985). *See Agostini*, 521 U.S. at 235–36 (overruling *Aguilar* in full and *Grand Rapids* in part).

Agostini that the Establishment Clause does not forbid publicly paid teachers from providing secular, remedial education on the premises of primary and secondary religious schools. As noted in our earlier discussion of *Aguilar* and *Grand Rapids*, the challenged aid extended to religious and nonreligious schools alike, and the purpose of the program— supporting secular education for those with special educational needs—readily satisfied the first prong of *Lemon*. Rejecting the contrary reasoning of its 1985 decisions, the Court in *Agostini* concluded that the aid program also survived the remainder of the *Lemon* analysis, now modified to relax the entanglement inquiry by merging it into the effect prong. In *Mitchell*, the Supreme Court likewise approved a program of aid that provided federally funded computers and other instructional equipment and materials to primary and secondary schools, religious as well as nonreligious, with the amount of aid dependent on the number of students at each school. As in *Agostini*, a secular purpose was clearly present, and the Court also found the effect analysis satisfied, even though this conclusion required it to overrule two additional precedents from the earlier doctrinal era.[123]

Agostini and *Mitchell* make it clear that even in the context of direct aid, programs that are formally nondiscriminatory are likely to be upheld. When "aid is allocated on the basis of neutral, secular

---

123. In *Mitchell*, the Court overruled its contrary holdings in *Meek v. Pittenger*, 421 U.S. 349 (1975), and *Wolman v. Walter*, 433 U.S. 229 (1977). *See Mitchell*, 530 U.S. at 808, 835 (plurality opinion); *id.* at 837 (O'Connor, J., concurring in the judgment).

criteria that neither favor nor disfavor religion, and is made available to both religious and secular beneficiaries on a nondiscriminatory basis," the Court wrote in *Agostini*, "the aid is less likely to have the effect of advancing religion." As with comparable programs of indirect aid, the Court reasoned, such programs do not "give aid recipients any incentive to modify their religious beliefs or practices" in order to qualify.[124] Here again, it seems that the Court believes that formal religious equality tends to promote substantive equality and religious voluntarism as well. Under the Court's reasoning, moreover, formally nondiscriminatory programs of aid do not have the effect of endorsing religion. Rather, they fully and equally respect the religious identity of all citizens, and, as a result, they do nothing to weaken the religious inclusiveness of the political community.

One might extend this reasoning to sanction all programs of aid that are formally nondiscriminatory. A four-justice plurality appeared to be moving in that direction in *Mitchell*,[125] and the plurality's view could find majority support in the future. At present, however, direct aid, even if formally nondiscriminatory, is subject to certain additional restrictions. Although the Court has not fully explained its reasoning, these additional restrictions might reflect structural constitutional values, both political and religious—protecting the government from potentially divisive religious involvement and protecting religion and the autonomy of religious organizations from the government's potentially unhelpful

124. *Agostini*, 521 U.S. at 231, 232.
125. *See Mitchell*, 530 U.S. at 801–36 (plurality opinion).

financial "help," which typically comes with strings attached. These structural values might support the separationist limits that the Court has continued to affirm even in the context of formally nondiscriminatory programs.

There appear to be four surviving Establishment Clause limits on formally nondiscriminatory programs of direct aid. These limits can be seen as remnants of the doctrinal approach of the 1970s and 1980s.

First, a program of direct aid cannot involve an unconstitutionally "excessive" entanglement between the government and religious organizations. Even after *Agostini* and *Mitchell*, for example, the government presumably cannot provide direct aid in a manner that includes a delegation of governmental power to religious organizations.[126] Under the Supreme Court's recent decisions, however, the entanglement limitation apparently is confined to extreme institutional entanglement. Routine administrative cooperation and governmental monitoring are no longer regarded as problematic.[127]

Second, the Court has suggested that the amount of direct aid to religious schools or organizations— at least if "pervasively sectarian"[128]—cannot be too

126. *Cf.* Larkin v. Grendel's Den, Inc., 459 U.S. 116 (1982) (holding that the government cannot grant churches, along with schools, the power to veto liquor licenses for nearby restaurants).

127. *See Agostini*, 521 U.S. at 232–34.

128. In *Mitchell*, a four-justice plurality argued that whether a religious organization is "pervasively sectarian" should not

substantial. In *Agostini*, for example, the Court emphasized that the publicly funded remedial education was "supplemental to the regular curricula" and therefore did not " 'reliev[e] sectarian schools of costs they otherwise would have borne in educating their students.' "[129]

Third, the Court has indicated that the substance of direct aid must be secular. More precisely, the aid must be segregated and confined to secular uses and cannot be diverted by its recipients to religious purposes. This point was emphasized by Justice O'Connor in her controlling opinion in *Mitchell*, in which she and Justice Breyer concurred only in the judgment, thereby limiting the reach of the Court's holding. Thus, Justices O'Connor and Breyer joined the plurality in concluding that the government can provide computers and other instructional equipment to religious schools, but they insisted that the schools cannot be allowed to use the equipment for religious purposes and that the government must establish adequate safeguards against this improper use.[130]

matter, not even in the context of direct aid, but this opinion did not command majority support. *See Mitchell*, 530 U.S. at 826–29 (plurality opinion).

129. *Agostini*, 521 U.S. at 228 (citation omitted).

130. *See Mitchell*, 530 U.S. at 840–44, 857–67 (O'Connor, J., concurring in the judgment). Even the plurality in *Mitchell* would have recognized a limit on the substance of public aid, but it would have required only that the content of the aid be secular at the time the government provides it. The plurality would not have precluded religious uses of the aid after it reached the hands of religious organizations. Accordingly, the plurality reasoned that it was permissible for the government to provide

Fourth, the Court has suggested that direct money payments (as opposed to in-kind support) to "pervasively sectarian" religious schools and organizations might be problematic even if the grants are restricted to secular uses. In *Agostini*, for instance, the Court noted that under the program it upheld, "No [government] funds ever reach the coffers of religious schools."[131] Conversely, the Court has permitted direct money payments to religious organizations that are not pervasively sectarian—including religiously affiliated colleges, universities, hospitals, and charities—as long as the grants are in fact restricted to secular uses.[132] Under this analysis, "charitable choice" programs calling for direct mon-

religious schools with computers and other instructional equipment—an entirely secular form of aid—even if the schools thereafter used the equipment for religious purposes. Conversely, the plurality indicated that it would preclude the government from providing the schools with Bibles or other religious materials as such. *See id.* at 820–25, 831–35 (plurality opinion).

131. *Agostini*, 521 U.S. at 228. *But cf.* Committee for Public Educ. & Religious Liberty v. Regan, 444 U.S. 646 (1980) (upholding direct cash reimbursement from state funds to religious schools for certain state-required testing and reporting activities); *Mitchell*, 530 U.S. at 818–20 & n.8 (plurality opinion) (noting that direct money payments raise special concerns, but questioning whether those concerns are enough to justify a distinctive Establishment Clause limitation).

132. *See, e.g.*, Roemer v. Board of Public Works, 426 U.S. 736 (1976); Bowen v. Kendrick, 487 U.S. 589 (1988); *cf. id.* at 624–25 (Kennedy, J., concurring) (arguing that grant money should be permitted to flow even to pervasively sectarian organizations as long as the money is not used to further religion); *see generally Mitchell*, 530 U.S. at 826–29 (plurality opinion) (contending that the Court should abandon the distinction between pervasively sectarian and other religious organizations).

ey grants might permissibly extend to religiously affiliated social-service providers, but perhaps not to providers that are pervasively sectarian.[133]

Given the trend favoring formal religious equality as the dominant constitutional value in this area and the Supreme Court's resulting inclination to approve formally nondiscriminatory programs of aid, it is not clear that these four Establishment Clause limits will continue to be recognized. Indeed, even as they stand, most of the limitations are not categorical, and the Court is likely to construe them in a relatively permissive fashion. Thus, the Court could readily uphold a challenged program by finding, for example, that any entanglement is not "excessive," that the aid to religious organizations is not unduly substantial, or that the religious recipients of direct money grants are not "pervasively" sectarian.

The most categorical of the four limitations is the requirement that direct aid must be segregated and

133. For comprehensive analysis of the constitutional and other legal issues raised by "charitable choice" and related initiatives, see Lupu & Tuttle, *supra* note 118 (along with the authors' annual updates to this report); Ira C. Lupu & Robert W. Tuttle, *The Faith–Based Initiative and the Constitution*, 55 DePaul L. Rev. 1 (2005).

Discretionary grant programs, calling for governmental officials to allocate public money selectively on the basis of case-by-case evaluations, may give rise to special Establishment Clause concerns. In particular, the granting of such awards to pervasively sectarian organizations might suggest purposeful religious discrimination in the grant-making process or, at least, the appearance of improper religious favoritism or endorsement. Indeed, these concerns might arise even if the discretionary awards provided not money, but in-kind support.

confined to secular uses and cannot be diverted by its recipients to religious purposes. If the plurality opinion in *Mitchell* were to become a majority view, however, this requirement would largely disappear.[134] Moreover, even as it stands, this limitation is subject to two significant and longstanding exceptions.

The first exception is direct aid in the form of tax exemptions. Thus, the Supreme Court has upheld the extension of tax exemptions to churches, synagogues, mosques, and other religious organizations, pervasively sectarian or otherwise, as part of a formally nondiscriminatory program of exemptions for nonprofit organizations in general. The financial benefit of this tax-exempt status is in no way segregated and confined to secular activities. Instead, it extends without limitation to the distinctively religious activities, including worship, of the churches and other religious organizations that qualify. Nonetheless, in its 1970 decision in *Walz v. Tax Commission*,[135] the Court found that this type of direct and unsegregated aid is constitutionally permissible, in part because it is highly traditional[136] and in part because the aid is negative, not affirmative. The tax exemption simply leaves the religious organizations untaxed, along with other nonprofit

134. *See supra* note 130 and accompanying text.

135. 397 U.S. 664 (1970).

136. This is not to suggest that tax exemptions, which provide tangible as opposed to merely symbolic support, could fit within the Court's implicit "tradition" exception to its usual Establishment Clause doctrine.

organizations.[137] For reasons discussed earlier in this chapter, this type of aid cannot be said to redress a substantial burden on religious exercise and therefore cannot be defended as a matter of permissible accommodation. But tax exemptions can be seen to limit the entanglement between religion and government, thereby promoting the structural values that are associated with institutional separation.

The second exception is direct aid in the form of access to public property for the purpose of engaging in religious speech. We already have discussed various aspects of the Supreme Court's "equal access" doctrine, both in earlier sections of this chapter and at the beginning of Chapter 5. To recapitulate, the Supreme Court has ruled in a series of cases that the Establishment Clause generally does not preclude the government from providing religious speakers with the same access to public property that it affords to other private speakers. In these cases, the Court has not only rejected the government's Establishment Clause argument for denying access, but it has further concluded that when the government has created a forum for a broad range of private expression, freedom of speech affirmatively demands that the religious speakers be given the equal access that they seek. Applying this reasoning, the Court has permitted—

137. Contrast *Texas Monthly, Inc. v. Bullock*, 489 U.S. 1 (1989), discussed earlier in this chapter. In *Texas Monthly*, the Court invalidated a sales tax exemption that was not general and nondiscriminatory, but that instead was limited to the sale of religious literature by religious organizations.

and required—the government to provide this formally nondiscriminatory aid to religious groups without in any way segregating and confining the aid to secular activities. Thus, the religious groups are provided with access to public property that they can use for prayer, worship, religious discussion, evangelism, and other distinctively religious activities.

This series of cases began in 1981 with the Supreme Court's decision in *Widmar v. Vincent*,[138] which permitted—and required—a state university to allow student religious groups to use the university's meeting rooms on the same basis as other student groups. Since *Widmar*, the Court has extended this analysis to the after-hours use of public school buildings by private religious groups, including those wishing to conduct after-school religious meetings for elementary students.[139] Notably, the Court also has ruled that formally nondiscriminatory access is sometimes permitted—and required—for public "property" in the form of aid beyond the provision of physical space. Thus, in its 1995 decision in *Rosenberger v. Rector and Visitors of the University of Virginia*,[140] the Court held that the

138. 454 U.S. 263 (1981).

139. *See* Lamb's Chapel v. Center Moriches Union Free School Dist., 508 U.S. 384 (1993); Good News Club v. Milford Central School, 533 U.S. 98 (2001); *see also* Board of Educ. of Westside Community Schools v. Mergens, 496 U.S. 226 (1990) (rejecting an Establishment Clause attack on the Equal Access Act of 1984, which provides statutory equal access rights for noncurricular student groups at public secondary schools).

140. 515 U.S. 819 (1995).

University of Virginia could not deny "student activities" financial support to a student religious group seeking payment for the cost of printing its Christian publication.

Rosenberger is a precedent of limited reach. The Court emphasized that the funding was broadly available to a diverse array of student groups, thereby creating a "metaphysical" forum for private expression.[141] It also noted, for example, that the funding was derived from student fees, not general tax money; that the university had disassociated itself from the student speech in question; that the university would be paying the third-party printer and would not be providing public money directly to the "coffers" of the religious group itself; and that the group was not a church or similar "religious institution" as such.[142] More generally, a majority of the Court has insisted that even with respect to physical space, equal access for religious speech is not permitted, not even in a public forum, if the context—for example, close proximity to the seat of government and the absence of an appropriate disclaimer of official sponsorship—would create the appearance of governmental endorsement.[143]

141. *Cf.* Locke v. Davey, 540 U.S. 712, 720 n.3 (2004) (holding that *Rosenberger* did not extend to a state-sponsored college scholarship program because the program was not designed to encourage a variety of private views and therefore was "not a forum for speech").

142. *See Rosenberger*, 515 U.S. at 828–46.

143. As noted earlier in this chapter, five justices expressed this view in their separate opinions in *Capitol Square Review*

Although the Court's equal access doctrine itself is subject to limitations, it represents an important exception to the Establishment Clause requirement that direct aid be segregated and confined to secular uses. This exception honors free speech principles, including especially the principle of viewpoint neutrality, and it therefore serves constitutional values that counterbalance the Establishment Clause values that might otherwise support the segregation requirement.

Constitutional Values and the Establishment Clause

As this lengthy chapter reveals, the Supreme Court's Establishment Clause decisionmaking is quite complex. At the level of general doctrine, the Court simultaneously recognizes three basic tests—the *Lemon* test, the endorsement test, and a coercion test—and, beyond that, it considers two additional general factors or concepts—tradition and accommodation. At a more specific level, the Court's doctrine includes separate strands, with differing points of analysis and emphasis, for religion and the public schools, religious symbolism in other contexts, and public aid to religious schools, organizations, and individuals. Both the Court's general doctrine and its particular decisions serve a variety

and Advisory Board v. Pinette, 515 U.S. 753 (1995). *See supra* note 89 and accompanying text.

of constitutional values, both individual and structural in nature. Indeed, one can find support for each of the constitutional values that we initially addressed in Chapter 3. Thus, in various and complicated ways, the Court's doctrine and decisions can be said to protect religious voluntarism, religious identity, and religious equality; to promote a religiously inclusive political community and to protect the government from improper religious involvement; to protect religion and the autonomy of religious institutions; and to preserve traditional governmental practices.

This complex picture, however, may be somewhat misleading. The Court's doctrine and decisions are indeed complex, but they also include common themes, and there is a powerful trend toward greater simplicity. Thus, the *Lemon* and endorsement tests, working together, provide the Court's general approach except when the discrete areas of tradition or accommodation are implicated. Under these tests, at least as they are understood today, the government generally is forbidden from conferring discriminatory benefits on religion, but it is generally free to extend nondiscriminatory benefits to religious beneficiaries, including religious organizations. More specifically, the conferral of benefits on religion typically is unconstitutional if, but only if, the government is formally or deliberately discriminating in religion's favor. Relatedly, the dominant constitutional value under the Establishment Clause is increasingly that of religious equality, understood in a strictly formal sense. Substantive religious equality and other constitutional values have not disappeared from view, but their role today is decidedly secondary, with the Court generally assuming that formal equality will tend to promote these other values as well.

CHAPTER 7

CONCLUDING OBSERVATIONS AND A GLANCE TO THE FUTURE

We began in Chapter 1 by highlighting the broad range of questions that arise from the seemingly simple command of the Religion Clauses: "Congress shall make no law respecting an establishment of religion, or prohibiting the free exercise thereof...." In Chapter 2, we considered the original understanding—not only of these provisions of the First Amendment, but also of the Fourteenth Amendment provisions that have been used to extend the Religion Clauses to the states. We concluded that the original understanding cannot support the Supreme Court's contemporary constitutional doctrine, which instead reflects a value-laden process of creative interpretation. Through this process of creative interpretation, the Court has identified and protected a variety of constitutional values, including values that are embedded in our political and cultural history and values that have emerged and evolved over time.

In an attempt to unearth these embedded and evolving values, Chapter 3 traced the historical development of American religious liberty from the founding to the present. Focusing on the contemporary period in the light of this history, we suggested that the Supreme Court's decisionmaking under the Religion Clauses has been influenced by at least six constitutional values or sets of values: religious voluntarism; respecting religious identity; religious equality; promoting a religiously inclusive political community and protecting government from improper religious involvement; protecting religion from government and protecting the autonomy of religious institutions; and preserving traditional governmental practices. This discussion set the stage for the next three chapters, which utilized these values in explaining and evaluating the many components of the Court's constitutional doctrine.

In Chapter 4, we addressed doctrinal fundamentals that are common to both the Free Exercise and Establishment Clauses. Chapter 5 considered the Supreme Court's Free Exercise doctrine, and Chapter 6 explored the Court's doctrine under the Establishment Clause. In these chapters, we confronted an array of constitutional problems, examined the Court's diverse responses, and noted the relative influence of particular constitutional values in various contexts. In so doing, we discovered that the Court's doctrine is complex and multifaceted, and that its relationship to constitutional values is both subtle and complicated.

Despite the complexity of the Supreme Court's doctrine, a common theme emerges from Chapters 4, 5, and 6. In recent years, under the Free Exercise and Establishment Clauses alike, the Court has emphasized the constitutional value of religious equality, and it increasingly has understood this value in formal rather than substantive terms. In Chapter 4, we introduced the basic proposition that formal or deliberate discrimination on the basis of religion is a critical touchstone under the Religion Clauses, regardless of whether the discrimination imposes a burden or confers a benefit. Chapter 5 elaborated this proposition in the context of the Free Exercise Clause, especially in discussing the doctrine of *Employment Division v. Smith*.[1] According to *Smith*, burdens on the exercise of religion generally are unconstitutional if, but only if, they are deliberately discriminatory.

As Chapter 6 revealed, the Supreme Court's Establishment Clause doctrine is far too complicated to be captured in a single theme. Even so, the Court's recent decisionmaking under the Establishment Clause, like that under the Free Exercise Clause, is driven heavily by the value of formal religious equality. Thus, the Court generally invalidates deliberately discriminatory benefits to religion even as it generally upholds the inclusion of religious beneficiaries in formally nondiscriminatory programs of aid. In recent cases exemplifying this pattern, the Court has followed past precedent in precluding the public schools from purposefully favoring religion,[2] and it has confirmed that the government likewise cannot purposefully promote religion through symbolic displays outside the public

1. 494 U.S. 872 (1990).

2. *See* Lee v. Weisman, 505 U.S. 577 (1992); Santa Fe Indep. Sch. Dist. v. Doe, 530 U.S. 290 (2000).

school context.[3] At the same time, the Court, relaxing prior doctrine, increasingly has upheld formally nondiscriminatory programs of aid, both direct and indirect, that extend to religious recipients.[4]

The trend toward formal equality brings increasing coherence to the Supreme Court's constitutional decisionmaking under the Religion Clauses. But this trend is not cost-free. Formal religious equality often promotes substantive religious equality and other constitutional values, but sometimes it does not. A single-minded focus on formal equality, therefore, inevitably sacrifices other constitutional values by denying them independent consideration.

The sacrifice of important constitutional values is apparent in the Free Exercise context. There, under *Smith*, the government generally is free to impose nondiscriminatory burdens on the exercise of religion, no matter how substantial the burdens might be. The approach of *Smith* promotes doctrinal clarity, but it seriously impairs religious voluntarism, religious identity, and other constitutional values.

In the Establishment Clause context, by contrast, the Supreme Court's increasing emphasis on formal religious equality seems more benign, and perhaps it is. More specifically, the inclusion of religious organizations in formally nondiscriminatory programs of aid may, as the Court believes, further not only formal equality but other constitutional values

3. *See* McCreary County v. ACLU of Ky., 545 U.S. 844 (2005).

4. *See, e.g.*, Agostini v. Felton, 521 U.S. 203 (1997); Mitchell v. Helms, 530 U.S. 793 (2000); Zelman v. Simmons–Harris, 536 U.S. 639 (2002).

as well. Even so, there are subtle but significant risks to religious liberty.[5]

Governmental programs of aid typically include conditions that the recipient organizations must honor. Under the school voucher program approved in *Zelman v. Simmons–Harris*,[6] for instance, participating schools were barred from discriminating on the basis of religion. This precluded religious schools from favoring members of their own religion—or even religious believers in general over atheists—in the admission of students and, apparently, also in the hiring of administrators and teachers.[7] Moreover, the strings attached to funding programs such as this can expand over time, even as the participating organizations become more and more dependent on the government's financial support. Although the financial support is a carrot, not a stick, it might nonetheless induce religious organizations to modify and weaken their religious practices and requirements in order to meet the government's demands. This prospect threatens important constitutional values: protecting religion from government and protecting the autonomy of religious institutions. Due to differences in theology and mission, moreover, the adverse impact might be greater

5. *See* Daniel O. Conkle, *The Path of American Religious Liberty: From the Original Theology to Formal Neutrality and an Uncertain Future*, 75 Ind. L.J. 1, 21–24 (2000).

6. 536 U.S. 639 (2002).

7. *See id.* at 712–13 (Souter, J., dissenting). Likewise, by implication, this prohibition appeared to forbid religious schools from requiring students or teachers to participate in prayer or other religious exercises.

for some religions than others, meaning that formal equality here might jeopardize substantive equality.[8]

The Supreme Court's elevation of formal religious equality to a central position reflects a particular understanding of evolving constitutional values. This understanding is driven by various philosophical, jurisprudential, and religious forces.[9] It is heavily influenced, for example, by the general emphasis on nondiscrimination in today's constitutional and legal culture, a culture that supports not only a vibrant Equal Protection doctrine, but nondiscrimination statutes of all sorts. The trend favoring formal equality is also a response to America's ever-increasing religious diversity, the bewildering array of potential claims under the Religion Clauses, and, as discussed in Chapter 4, the increasingly difficult problem of defining "religion" for the purpose of evaluating such claims. To the extent that the Court limits itself to formal equality and the principle of nondiscrimination, the Court need only determine whether "religion" has been targeted for formal or deliberate discrimination. This does not eliminate the definitional problem, but it does reduce its significance by narrowing and simplifying the constitutional doctrine to which it relates. More generally, a constitutional doctrine stressing formal

8. For a discussion of these problems in the context of "charitable choice" programs, see Daniel O. Conkle, *Religion, Politics, and the 2000 Presidential Election: A Selective Survey and Tentative Appraisal*, 77 Ind. L.J. 247, 249–52 (2002).

9. For elaboration beyond that offered here, see Conkle, *supra* note 5, at 25–36.

equality and nondiscrimination supports contemporary policies of judicial restraint and federalism. Thus, it limits the role of the federal judiciary by emphasizing a relatively clear-cut, rule-based approach to constitutional questions even as it tends to encourage judicial deference to majoritarian governmental policies, most of which are the product of state law.

Judicial restraint and federalism, of course, are constitutional values in their own right, values linked not so much to the Religion Clauses as to broader, structural considerations. As we have just noted, these values support the Supreme Court's increasing emphasis on formal religious equality. At the same time, they also help explain some of the Court's departures from this trend. In particular, the Court sometimes has found that formal equality is constitutionally permissible but not constitutionally required.[10] In so doing, the Court has deferred to the majoritarian political process, finding that "there is room for play in the joints" between the Free Exercise and Establishment Clauses.[11]

Under *Employment Division v. Smith*, for example, formal equality generally is sufficient under the Free Exercise Clause, but the Establishment Clause doctrine of permissible accommodation gives Con-

10. *See* Douglas Laycock, *Substantive Neutrality Revisited*, 110 W. Va. L. Rev. 51, 60–64 (2007). Adapting Professor Laycock's phrasing to reflect the terminology we are using here, this approach can be described as "permissive formal [equality]— formal [equality] is permitted but some alternative is also permitted." *Id.* at 61. (Laycock uses the word "neutrality" instead of "equality.")

11. *See* Locke v. Davey, 540 U.S. 712, 718 (2004); Cutter v. Wilkinson, 544 U.S. 709, 713, 719 (2005).

gress and the states considerable leeway to provide religion-based exemptions if they choose.[12] Likewise, in the context of public aid, formal equality—extending nondiscriminatory support to religious and nonreligious recipients alike—usually is enough to satisfy the Establishment Clause, but under *Locke v. Davey*'s interpretation of the Free Exercise Clause,[13] religion-based, discriminatory funding exclusions are sometimes permissible. As discussed in Chapter 6, the doctrine of permissible accommodation permits Congress and the states to promote religious voluntarism, substantive religious equality, and other Free Exercise values that the Supreme Court itself is not protecting under *Smith*. By contrast, as discussed in Chapter 5, *Locke v. Davey*, whatever its scope, permits the states (and perhaps Congress) to discriminate against religion in a manner that frustrates those same Free Exercise values. *Locke* thus suggests that the Court sometimes is willing to privilege judicial restraint and federalism over the values of the Religion Clauses, including even the formal equality that the Court itself has championed. More generally, the Court's decision-making, taken as a whole, tends to favor formal religious equality but also deference to the political process, a stance that advances the values of judicial restraint and federalism.[14]

12. *See* Corporation of the Presiding Bishop v. Amos, 483 U.S. 327 (1987); *Cutter*, 544 U.S. 709.

13. *See Locke*, 540 U.S. 712.

14. Beyond its substantive interpretations of the Religion Clauses, the Supreme Court can promote deference to the politi-

The Supreme Court's membership recently has changed, with Chief Justice Roberts replacing Chief Justice Rehnquist and Justice Alito replacing Justice O'Connor. These changes are unlikely to affect the Court's Free Exercise doctrine.[15] Conversely, should the issues return to the Court, two plurality opinions under the Establishment Clause could become majority holdings—assuming that Chief Justice Roberts takes the same view as his predecessor and Justice Alito adopts a different position than Justice O'Connor.

These potential Establishment Clause shifts, if they occur, would further advance the existing trend favoring formal equality combined with defer-

cal process by vigorously enforcing the procedural prerequisites for federal court jurisdiction, including the requirement that challengers have proper standing to sue, especially in Establishment Clause cases. For recent decisions of this type, not yet indicating a trend but suggestive of that possibility, see Elk Grove Unified Sch. Dist. v. Newdow, 542 U.S. 1 (2004) (holding that a parent with limited and disputed custodial rights lacked "prudential standing" to challenge the "under God" language in public school recitations of the Pledge of Allegiance); Hein v. Freedom from Religion Foundation, Inc., __ U.S. __, 127 S.Ct. 2553 (2007) (rejecting taxpayer standing in an Establishment Clause challenge to executive branch expenditures funded by general as opposed to specific congressional appropriations).

15. Notably, Justice Alito, as a circuit judge, authored an opinion granting Free Exercise protection under a robust interpretation of *Smith*'s requirement of "general applicability." *See* Fraternal Order of Police v. City of Newark, 170 F.3d 359 (3d Cir. 1999). But even if Justice Alito would vote to abandon the restrictive approach of *Smith* altogether, in favor of a return to earlier doctrine, his position would be no different than that of Justice O'Connor. *See* Employment Div. v. Smith, 494 U.S. 872, 891–903 (1990) (O'Connor, J., concurring in the judgment).

ence to the political process. Thus, the plurality opinion in *Mitchell v. Helms*[16] could become a majority holding, further extending the permissible scope of nondiscriminatory public aid by permitting direct aid to religious organizations without the existing requirement that such aid be segregated and confined to secular uses and not be diverted by its recipients to religious purposes.[17] And the plurality opinion in *Van Orden v. Perry*,[18] if adopted by a majority, would permit the government (at least in many circumstances) to promote "passive" religious symbolism outside the public school setting, including displays of the Ten Commandments such as those invalidated in *McCreary County v. ACLU of Kentucky*.[19] Adopting the *Mitchell* plurality opinion would promote formal religious equality as well as deference to the political process. Adopting the plurality's view in *Van Orden*, by contrast, would honor deference to the political process but not formal religious equality, because it would permit the government (to some extent) to purposefully advance

16. 530 U.S. 793 (2000).

17. *See id.* at 801–36 (plurality opinion).

18. 545 U.S. 677 (2005).

19. 545 U.S. 844 (2005). The *Van Orden* plurality suggested that the Court generally should approve "passive" religious symbolism, at least if the symbolism has secular as well as religious significance. *See Van Orden*, 545 U.S. at 686–92 (plurality opinion). And the same four justices dissented in *McCreary*, making it appear that they would sanction virtually any Ten Commandments display (outside the public school setting). *See McCreary*, 545 U.S. at 900–12 (Scalia, J., joined by Rehnquist, C.J., and by Thomas and Kennedy, JJ., dissenting).

and endorse religion over irreligion.[20] It would be like *Locke v. Davey*, but with the deference here permitting discrimination in religion's favor.

Although other constitutional values have not disappeared from view, today's dominant values—formal religious equality on the one hand, judicial restraint and federalism on the other—have eclipsed, to a degree, other and competing values that the Religion Clauses can be understood to promote. In the near-term future, the Supreme Court is unlikely to reverse course, and it may push further along the path it recently has charted. In the longer term, however, the meaning of the Religion Clauses will continue to evolve. Perhaps, in some future period, the Court will reduce its reliance on formal equality and deference to the political process. It might return to earlier doctrinal frameworks, which gave greater weight to other values, or it might adopt new approaches that we cannot now anticipate. In any event, the Supreme Court's doctrine will undoubtedly change in the future, as it has in the past, and this change—whatever its direction—will inevitably reflect some combination of embedded and evolving constitutional values.

20. Such a decision plainly would depart from the test of *Lemon v. Kurtzman*, 403 U.S. 602 (1971), and also from the endorsement test, perhaps heralding a broader role for some version of a coercion test. Notably, however, such a development might not threaten the Court's public school precedents, because in that context the Court might continue to follow the "indirect coercion" reasoning of *Lee v. Weisman*, 505 U.S. 577 (1992).

TABLE OF CASES

References are to Pages.

INDEX

References are to Pages.

231

ORIGINAL UNDERSTANDING—Cont'd
Virginia's pre-constitutional experience, Supreme Court's selective focus on, 7–16

RELIGION CLAUSES IN GENERAL
      Generally, 1–4, 50 et seq.
Definition of "religion," 61–69, 114–15, 147, 151–52, 221
Disputes within religious organizations, 70–71, 107–08
Impermissible burdens and impermissible benefits, 50–55
"Incorporation" of Religion Clauses into Fourteenth Amendment, 10, 22–26
Interpretive methodology, "originalist" and "nonoriginalist," 2–3, 16–18, 29–30
Judicial inquiries into content and sincerity of religious beliefs, 69–72
Nondiscrimination as general principle under both clauses, 55–61
Relationship between two clauses
          generally, 50–52, 55–58, 97–101, 111–12, 114–16, 121, 123–24, 125n, 129, 139–54, 161–62, 163–64, 200–01, 222–23
    "play in the joints" between clauses, 98–100, 222–23
Sectarian and nonsectarian discrimination, 54–55, 56–59

RELIGIOUS FREEDOM STATUTES AND LEGISLATION
      Generally, 108–12, 150–52
Religious Freedom Restoration Act of 1993 (RFRA), 108–10, 111, 150–52
Religious Land Use and Institutionalized Persons Act of 2000 (RLUIPA), 110–12, 150–52
Religious Liberty Protection Act (RLPA) (proposed), 110
State statutes and legislation, 111, 150–52

STATE CONSTITUTIONAL LAW
Exemptions of religious conduct from legal burdens, 142
Prohibitions on aid to religion, 98, 201n

TRENDS IN SUPREME COURT
Emphasis on formal religious equality and nondiscrimination, 59–61, 112–13, 214–15, 217–22
Emphasis on judicial restraint and federalism, 98–100, 222–23
Supreme Court's recent membership changes, possible impact of, 224–26

✝